Topics in Autism

Second Edition

Siblings
of **Children** with
Autism

A Guide for Families

Sandra L. Harris, Ph.D. and
Beth A. Glasberg, Ph.D.

Sandra L. Harris, Ph.D, *series editor*

Woodbine House ◆ 2003

© 2003 Sandra L. Harris and Beth A. Glasberg
Second Edition

All rights reserved under International and Pan-American copyright conventions.
Published in the United States of America by Woodbine House, Inc., 6510 Bells Mill
Rd., Bethesda, MD 20817. 800-843-7323. www.woodbinehouse.com

Library of Congress Cataloging-in-Publication Data

Harris, Sandra L.
   Siblings of children with autism : a guide for families / Sandra L. Harris and
Beth A. Glasberg.—2nd ed.
   p. cm.
Includes bibliographical references and index.
   ISBN 1-890627-29-1 (pbk.)
   1. Autistic children—Family relationships. 2. Brothers and sisters—Family
relationships. 3. Brothers and sisters—Mental health. 4. Family. I. Glasberg, Beth
A. II. Title.

RJ506.A9H27 2003
649'.154—dc21
                                                                2003001239

Manufactured in the United States of America

10 9 8 7 6 5 4 3 2 1

For Jay and for Deedee

Who, as our siblings,
taught us a great deal
about life, love,
and the joys of connection

TABLE OF CONTENTS

Preface vii

Chapter 1 Brothers and Sisters: Getting Together
and Getting Along 1

Chapter 2 He Doesn't Know What Angels Are:
Autism Viewed through Children's Eyes 27

Chapter 3 Why Does He Do That?
Explaining Autism to Children 53

Chapter 4 Let's Talk: Helping Children Share Their
Thoughts and Feelings 79

Chapter 5 The Balancing Act: Finding Time for
Family, Work, and Yourself 103

Chapter 6 Children at Play: Helping Children
Play Together 127

Chapter 7 An Adult Perspective: The Mature Sibling ... 149

Resource Guide 169

References 173

Index 177

PREFACE

Between the two of us, we have spent more than forty years serving children, adolescents, and adults with autism and their families. That privilege has given us the rare opportunity to come to know the many parents, grandparents, brothers, and sisters who lovingly surround the lives of people with autism. We have visited their homes, shared their joys and their tragedies, watched the brothers and sisters mature into fine adults, and, over the years, sometimes mourned their family losses. Life in a family that includes a child with autism is much like life in any other family, with an added challenge of helping the person with autism flourish in an often baffling world.

The treatment of disorders on the autism spectrum has made important advances in the past three decades. We know a great deal more about how to help people with autism achieve their potential than ever before. Some children are now able to function independently in a fully integrated classroom, others can be there with special support, while some children, in spite of all of our advances, continue to need a great deal of support in order to learn. All of these children have made far greater progress than would have been possible in years past, although our teaching technology still does not allow many of them to fully move beyond their neurological challenges.

Families of children with autism are confronted by the intense time demands of caring for their child with autism and struggling to meet their other family and life obligations as well. Particularly when a family has a home-based program for their young child, the time demands may seem endless and the challenge of caring for their other children may feel particularly daunting. Even when a child with autism is enrolled in a center-based program or is attending school full-time and the family has extra support from an extended family or from good friends, the task remains substantial and impacts on every aspect of family life.

As parents have shared these burdens with us, they have often spoken movingly of their concern for the other children in their family. What is it like to grow up as the sibling of a child with autism? How can parents help a child cope with the demands of this experience?

When we meet with the children themselves in sibling support groups, we hear their own concerns. From the younger children, there are sometimes puzzled questions about what is wrong with their brother or sister with autism or comments about how unfair they feel their parents are not to discipline their siblings the same way as themselves. From adolescents, we hear some of the most poignant concerns about their future and that of their sibling. These teens wonder if they will be expected to care for their brother or sister in the future. And some of them wonder about a possible genetic link in autism and what it means for them and any future children of their own. All of these questions are important ones that parents want to be able to answer for their children.

We hope that this book will be useful to parents of children with autism all along the spectrum, of all ages, in thinking about the needs of all of their family members. We also hope it will be useful to the professionals who serve them. We have tried to address some of the very compelling questions that parents and siblings have raised with us.

If you find this book useful, perhaps you will write to us and let us know. Many parents did that in response to the first edition and their suggestions have guided some of our revisions for this second edition. The most obvious change is the addition of a chapter on the concerns of adult siblings of people with autism, but there are also other comments scattered through the book that have grown directly from the input of parents. Just as the challenges of autism continue into adulthood for many people, so too do the challenges that go along with being a sibling.

We offer a special thanks to all of the siblings and their families who so generously shared their time, thoughts, and feelings about growing up with a brother or sister with autism. Their willingness to support our research effort has helped move the understanding of the lives of siblings ahead in important ways.

Although the two of us take responsibility for the content of this book, we also want to acknowledge the many families and individuals who supported us in its writing. Susan Stokes and Irvin Shapell at Woodbine House transformed our professional words into the user-friendly version you have before you. We both consider it a privilege to have our work published by a company that shares our commitment to serving parents of children with disabilities.

A number of parents contributed comments for the end section of each chapter or the photographs of children that brighten the pages. We have slightly changed some of the content to disguise the identity of the families involved, but we have not altered their intent. Our heartfelt thanks to each of the following families for their generosity: the Barsi Family, the Brown Family, the Conley Family, the Cuccia Family, the Glasberg-Katz Family, the Harris-Zuckerman Family, the Fogarty Family, the Denholtz-Melnitsky Family, the Kutchaver Family, the Maher Family, the M'Geehan Family, the Patel Family, the Ritchie Family, the Rogers Family, the Scannelli Family, the Silverman Family, the Sussman Family, the Weiss Family, and the Zadroga Family.

Our colleagues at the Douglass Developmental Disabilities Center, Jan Handleman, Maria Arnold, Marlene Brown, Marlene Cohen, Lara Delmolino, Rita Gordon, Barbara Kristoff, Donna Sloan, and Mary Jane Weiss have been uniformly supportive of our work and each of them excels in her/his own domain. We thank Jean L. Burton, Ph.D., who, as chair of the Douglass College Psychology Department, supported the creation of the Center more than thirty years ago.

Sandra also wishes to thank Joseph Masling, her graduate school mentor and now an enduring friend, for his unflagging support of her career. She also thanks Han van den Blink for teaching her how to think about individuals within the context of their family.

Beth knows that this book would not be possible without the help and support of her husband and family, whose immeasurable assistance, patience, and encouragement is deeply and greatly appreciated.

New Brunswick, New Jersey
Spring 2003

1 | Brothers and Sisters: Getting Together and Getting Along

The McGuire Family

Bang! The screen door slammed. Thump, thump, thump! Small feet ran hard up the hallway stairs to the second floor. Thud! The bedroom door slammed shut. Shortly the sounds of loud music erased all traces of silence in the McGuire household. Sally McGuire sighed deeply and shook her head. Something was bothering ten-year-old Kevin. But it was harder and harder to know what the boy was thinking or feeling. He was getting increasingly moody. Sometimes he was still a little boy who liked to cuddle with her, but more often now he held his distance. Her little adolescent!

Sally had little time to be lost in reverie. Her younger son, Mitch, was tugging at her leg. "Want juice." Her face brightened. "Great talking, Mitch," said Sally as she moved to the refrigerator and found his favorite drink.

Mitch was five this month, and a couple of years ago Sally had despaired that he would ever speak. She and her hus-

band, Tom, had gone from one specialist to another seeking an answer to the puzzle of their son's behavior. Finally, when Mitch was nearly three, they had found a psychologist who understood him. She had told the McGuires as gently as she could that Mitch had a developmental condition called Autistic Disorder. He would require years of intensive education to reach his potential and would probably require some special services all of his life.

Sally and Tom, although dismayed about Mitch's diagnosis, were relieved to finally know what was happening to him, and grateful to know how to help him. Soon they enrolled Mitch in a good preschool class and were immersed in home programming that required them to become very skillful teachers for Mitch. Their hard, time-consuming work was paying off in important changes in his behavior. He spoke now and had pretty much stopped his tantrums. He also seemed happier than they had ever known him.

The front doorbell rang. It was the McGuires' next-door neighbor, Rosemary Vandenbeck, who had known the McGuires for nearly ten years and had been a wonderful source of support with Mitch. Rosemary looked concerned. "Is Kevin around?" she asked. Sally said he was in his room. Rosemary went on to share with Sally what she had overheard in her backyard just a few minutes before Kevin had gone pounding up the stairs.

Kevin had been sitting on the back steps talking with Rosemary's boy, Jon. Their words drifted through the open window to where Rosemary was seated at her computer. The word "autism" caught her ear and she paused for a minute to listen. Kevin was telling Jon that he had a secret thought about his brother, Mitch. Sometimes he wished Mitch wasn't his brother, but that Jon was. His parents thought every little thing Mitch did was great, but they never paid any attention to what Kevin did. Sometimes he wondered if they really loved him as much as they loved Mitch. He knew Mitch had autism, but that didn't mean he should be able to get away with anything he wanted. Kevin felt like he had to be extra good at everything to make up for what Mitch could not do. None of it was fair!

As she heard this story from Rosemary, Sally felt an ache for Kevin, who had been bearing all his pain without saying a word.

And then she felt alarm because she had not understood Kevin well enough to see how bothered he was. Something had to be done, but how could she reach a son who seemed so remote?

Introduction

Kevin McGuire's feelings about his brother, Mitch, are not unusual. Many children in his situation have had times when they felt that their parents loved them less than they did their sibling with autism. Neither is his difficulty sharing his feelings with his parents unusual. It is not easy for many children to tell their parents their concerns about their brother or sister with autism.

Several things may be contributing to Kevin's silence. These include his sense of shame about his jealousy, his frustration that his parents are often busy with Mitch and do not seem to have much time for him, and his own beginning entry to adolescence, with a normal, gradual withdrawal from the world of the family to the world of peers. Each of these factors can, and probably do, contribute to Kevin's silence.

Do problems like those faced by the McGuire family mean that the barriers between parents and children are too high for good communication about a brother or sister with autism? Thankfully, they do not. Although the quality of family communication varies across time and across the developmental stages of a child's life, parents and children need not lose touch with one another about the important things in their lives. But good communication does not always come easily, and sometimes requires extra effort from everyone in the family.

This chapter summarizes some of what social scientists know about the relationships between typically developing siblings. It then examines the effect on these normal patterns of behavior when one of the children in the family has autism or a similar disorder. This chapter will help you understand the many different healthy ways children can learn to get along with each other. Chapter 2 reports the findings from a research project that looked

closely at how children's understanding of autism changes as they grow up. Chapter 3 describes how you can take developmental changes into account in deciding what kind of information you might share with your child about autism. Chapter 4 takes a look at what you can do to increase family communication. Chapter 5 examines some of the specific things you can do to help your children cope with the special needs of their brother or sister with autism. We will consider how the entire family can strike a healthy balance between inclusion and separateness, so that the needs of each family member are met as well as possible. Chapter 6 focuses on helping children become playmates for a sibling with autism. This chapter includes suggestions for teaching play skills to your children. The final chapter, Chapter 7, considers what enduring impact the experience of growing up with a brother or sister with autism has on an adult.

Special Family Circumstances

We wrote this book from the perspective of a family that consists of two parents and their biological children. However, we understand that many other healthy combinations are possible in families including adopted children, stepchildren, and foster children, and in single parent families. We hope that these families too will find much that is useful in our book.

Having worked with the many varied family constellations, we believe that most of the information we are offering will be useful for every family regardless of its structure. However, the single parent who must raise a child with autism without a supportive partner or the stepparent or stepchild who must learn to become part of an established family and take on responsibilities for a child with autism encounter special demands. For example, a typically developing stepchild not only has to learn to accept a new stepparent, but is cast into the role of sibling of a child with autism. Both the stepparent and stepchild may feel overwhelmed by these new roles.

Similarly, when the sibling relationship is based not on biology, but on adoption, family members will have questions of adoption to deal with, as well as the difficulties created by one child's autism. Some families elect to adopt a child with autism and others discover the disability after the adoption is final. In either case, the fact of adoption is an additional variable that can affect the family both positively and negatively (Brodzinsky & Schechter, 1990).

Any one of these challenges—being a single parent, stepparent, foster parent, or adoptive parent—places special demands on a person. When the needs of a child with autism are added to these basic family demands, some families may find that they would benefit from professional consultations to address the many issues they face. This might be with a psychologist, psychiatrist, social worker, family therapist, or a religious advisor who has had training in pastoral counseling. It helps if this professional has worked with people with autism. One way to find such a person may be through your local Autism Society of America (ASA) chapter. Other families who have had a good therapy experience, a child's teacher, or a pediatrician may also be good referral sources.

See Table 1 on the next page for a list of some of the professionals who provide support services for families and their children with autism. As discussed in Chapter 5, it is important to ask for help from family or professional helpers when you encounter tough problems in raising your child with autism.

Table 1-1 | Professionals Who May Be Able to Help

Clinical Psychologist. Has a doctorate in psychology and is licensed or certified by state. Clinical psychologists study human behavior and mental processes with the goal of reducing suffering and increasing self-understanding and healthy functioning. May work in public agency or private practice. Does behavioral intervention with child, parent training, diagnosis, and individual, marital, or family therapy. Provides consultation for finding community resources.

Family Therapist. May be a social worker, psychologist, psychiatrist, pastoral counselor, or marriage and family therapist who specializes in work with families.

Neurologist. Has an MD degree with specialized training in brain function. Provides consultation regarding diagnosis, medication, and community resources.

Psychiatrist. Has an MD degree with special training in psychiatry. Because of their medical training, psychiatrists have specialized, in-depth understanding of the biological factors underlying human behavior and have the expertise to prescribe medication and other medical treatments. Provides consultation

Another sometimes overlooked factor that may make life more difficult for the family of a child with autism is that there is an increased incidence of developmental disorders in siblings. We know, for example, that siblings of children with autism have a greater risk of reading difficulties and speech delays. Similar problems are identified in some parents of children with autism and highlight the genetic factors that play a role in some families (Folstein & Rosen-Sheidley, 2001).

One family we knew had one child with autism, another with a learning disability, and a third who was developing without any evident problems. Another family had three children on the autism spectrum, with one child who was significantly af-

regarding diagnosis, medication, and community resources. May do individual, marital, or family therapy.

School Psychologist. Has a master's degree or doctorate in school psychology. Licensed or certified by the state. May work in schools, public agencies, or private practice. Provides consultation regarding diagnosis, behavioral intervention for the child, parent training, resources in community, and individual, marital, or family therapy.

Special Education Teacher. Has a bachelor's or master's degree in education. Licensed by the state. Works in school setting. Provides consultation regarding behavioral intervention with the child, parent training, and resources in community.

Board Certified Behavior Analyst. Has passed a national examination in applied behavior analysis reflecting a mastery of how to apply the principles of learning to changing human behavior. May come from different helping professions, including psychology, speech, and special education. Has received extensive classroom and hands-on supervised training in the use of the techniques of applied behavior analysis. May work in schools, private agencies, or private practice. Provides consultation in the development of teaching programs and behavior management programs for people with autism.

fected by autism and two others whose symptoms were milder. These parents spent a great deal of time shuttling back and forth from one special program to another, and from one doctor's office to the next. Trying to balance their family needs eventually led one of couples into marital therapy in an effort to bring order to the chaos.

Fortunately, most siblings of children with autism do not have learning or language problems, and when they do, they are not as challenged as the child with autism. However, when these problems are present, siblings will need considerable help if they are to meet their potential. Under these circumstances, you will have your hands full meeting the special needs of two or more children and helping them develop their sibling relationship as well. Because of the increased risk of developmental problems, it makes sense to seek professional help if you suspect that one of your other children has a speech delay or other learning problem.

Siblings Across a Lifetime

Brothers and sisters are not just siblings in childhood. These relationships, at least in their formal sense, continue across our lifetime. For many adults, the person who has known us longest and best is our sibling. However, the quality of sibling relationships varies widely, and some of us are blessed with a sense of intimacy in our interactions with our brother or sister, while others of us hardly know this person with whom we share a profound biological bond. Although we choose our friendships, our brothers and sisters are imposed on us, and even if we are emotionally distanced from them, they remain part of the fabric of our lives.

In thinking about how your children get along with each other, it is helpful to understand that there are a variety of styles of sibling relationships that are "normal." You should also know that sibling relationships change as children grow up. There is no single prescription for how brothers and sisters should get along.

The Sibling Bond

In 1982, psychologists Stephen Bank and Michael Kahn studied the sibling bond through extensive interviews of several hundred siblings of different ages, gender, and social circumstances. They found that a process called "access" is one of the factors that creates an emotional bond between children. High access, with strong sibling bonds, is most likely to occur when children are close in age, of the same gender, and have shared many activities. Not surprisingly, low access with subsequent weaker bonds, often occurs when children are widely separated in age, have spent relatively little time together, and are of different gender. It is not essential that siblings share these qualities to form a strong bond, but they increase the likelihood of such a strength of connection.

It is worth noting that a strong bond does not always mean a happy bond. A strong sibling bond can be warm and loving, but also can be negative and tension filled (Bank and Kahn, 1982). The sense of connection between siblings can be a source of joy or of pain.

Early Childhood

The interaction between siblings changes as children grow up. A good relationship at age five will be different at age fifteen. Nonetheless, the groundwork for connection is laid down in early childhood. Warmth and affection early in childhood lay the foundation for intimacy and caring later on.

One of the first things you might wonder about siblings in early childhood is how an older child will react to the birth of a baby brother or sister, and the experience of "sib-ling rivalry." Many things change when a baby is born. For example, the birth of a younger brother or sister means a change in your relationship with your other child. You can no longer devote all your energies to that child. That change in attention often produces at least temporary behavior problems for the older child, including difficulties with toileting, withdrawal, aggressiveness, dependency, and anxiety (Cicirelli, 1995).

However, in spite of their transient discomfort, most children adjust well to a new baby. The role of parents is crucial in this adjustment. How you talk to your child about the baby is important in how the two of them will get along (Cicirelli, 1995). Children need support and reassurance that they are still loved, respected, and special, while they learn to live with the new little stranger in their lives. It is easy for adults to underestimate the impact on a child when a baby enters the family.

The process of change in sibling relationships continues year by year. Older siblings often act as models of behavior, will typically be the leaders in play with their brother or sister, and can be a source of security for the younger child (Cicirelli, 1995).

One of the important transitions in the interactions of brothers and sisters happens when the younger child is between three and four years of age. By this age, children have skills that make them increasingly desirable companions for childhood play. These skills include complex language, motor abilities, and a social repertoire that make them attractive playmates for their older brother or sister. As a result, the older child (if he is typically developing) begins to take an increasing interest in the younger (Dunn, 1992). By this age, the possibilities for both companionship and competition begin to emerge and the range of potential sibling interactions grows increasingly rich and complex. Young children who are closer together in age are likely to experience more quarrels and tension than children who are four or more years apart (Buhrmester, 1992), but they are also likely to develop a closer emotional bond.

The overall quality of family life has an important impact on how siblings get along with one another. Parents who have a good marriage and effectively resolve differences between themselves are more likely to have children who can do the same. Similarly, parents who are effective caretakers for their children are likely to have children who relate well to one another (Boer, Goedhart, & Treffers, 1992). Being an effective parent includes such qualities as:

- conveying respect, warmth, and love,
- being consistent in one's expectations and rules,
- setting clear limits on children's inappropriate behaviors, and

■ providing predictable but flexible childhood routines.

In families where there are serious parental problems, siblings can be an important source of support for one another (Jenkins, 1992), but these relationships cannot replace the love and wisdom of a competent parent. These findings highlight how essential it is that every parent develop good parenting skills, whether you form a two parent, or a single parent family. Feeling comfortable with yourself and having good relationships with other people is important not only for yourself, but for your children as well.

Middle Childhood and Adolescence

Changes in sibling interactions continue in middle childhood, from about nine to twelve years of age. Judy Dunn (1992), an expert on sibling relationships, reports that during middle childhood there is an important change in how siblings get along. This is a time when the interactions between children become more equal and balanced. During early childhood most of the caretaking between siblings flows from the older to the  younger child. However, when the younger sibling reaches eleven or twelve years of age, the older sibling does less nurturing, creating a more balanced relationship between the children.

In addition to the shift in caretaking, there is also a shift in dominance, with the younger child achieving a more equal footing with the older by about twelve years of age. This greater equity in caretaking and power may benefit both children. The younger child has reached an age of increased independence, and the older child is no longer responsible for looking after the younger and may have more freedom to pursue adolescent goals (Buhrmester, 1992). Although many siblings report a relatively high level of conflict with their brother or sister during preadolescence and early adolescence, by middle to late adolescence there is a marked decline in this tension (Buhrmester, 1992).

During early and middle childhood and preadolescence, parents and siblings are the most important sources of emotional support and sharing for their children. Parents play the central support role for children until sixth or seventh grade. They help their children solve problems, comfort their distress, and share a range of activities and interests. However, after that age, family members decline in importance, as friends and romantic relationships grow in meaning (Buhrmester, 1992). This does not mean that the family becomes unimportant, but there is a shift in the balance of relationships so that those outside of the home are an increasing source of support. This shift is part of the developmental process that enables children to become competent, independent adults in Western culture.

Adulthood

Sibling relationships can remain important throughout our lives. With increasingly smaller family size, longer life spans, and a greater probability of divorce and remarriage, the sibling relationship may be more important today than it was one hundred years ago (Bank & Kahn, 1982). Friendships may be lost in moves, marriages dissolve, and parents die, but the sibling relationship may endure through all of these transitions. In old age our brother or sister may remain the sole link with our past.

When a Brother or Sister Has Autism

What happens to the normal course of sibling relationships when one of the children has autism and is unable to respond in the usual fashion to the joy, the play, and the rough and tumble of childhood? It is easy to imagine the frustration and disappointment a girl feels when her sister shows no interest in playing childhood games. [After a while, she will probably give up trying to relate to her and focus her energy on other people. The sibling relationship may become one of sadness or indifference.]

A school-aged child will be understandably angry if his brother with autism comes into his room and destroys a model airplane that he has labored over for several days. [Children of any age may begin to doubt their worth and importance when their parents seem preoccupied with their sibling with autism and appear to have no time for them.] We saw a vivid example of this in the case of Kevin and Mitch McGuire. Kevin resented the time his parents spent with Mitch and wondered if they loved Mitch more than him.

Of course, these kinds of frustration are not unique to families where there is a child with autism. Most of us have been angry at our brother or sister, and there are few of us who never felt that our sibling was getting more parental attention than he or she deserved. So, it is important to recognize the difference between the normal frustration of childhood and the special impact of having a sibling with autism or a related developmental disability. Some of these differences are discussed later in this chapter.

[You will find it reassuring that the research shows that most children who have a sibling with autism learn to handle the experience and show no major ill effects] (e.g., Grissom, & Borkowski, 2002; McHale, Sloan, & Simeonsson, 1986). Nonetheless, there are special demands growing up in a household where one child has autism. Although some children learn to deal with these demands, others have greater difficulty. While serious behavior problems rarely arise when a child has a sibling with autism, brothers and sisters do have to grapple with the special demands imposed on them. If you understand these demands, you may be able to ease your child's burden. Ultimately, if things go better for your child, they will go better for you as well.

Older Sisters/Younger Brothers

Early research on siblings' experiences looked mainly at things such as birth order (first born, middle, or last), and age and gender of the child with a developmental disability and the typically developing siblings. For example, older sisters and younger brothers of children with developmental disabilities were sometimes found to be at greater risk for emotional problems than other children (Seligman & Darling, 1997). However, this relationship between age and gender is complicated, not well understood, and does not always occur. Furthermore, even if we knew that these two groups of children were at greater risk for difficulties, we would still not know much about the specific emotional or behavior problems bothering them. Although the early research highlighted some potential trouble spots, it did not tell us much about what was actually going on in families that made some children very unhappy, while in other families children coped well.

More recently, researchers have looked in greater detail at the experience of growing up with a brother or sister who has a developmental disability. For example, psychologist Susan McHale and her colleagues found that children between the ages of six and fifteen had mostly positive things to say about their brother or sister, regardless of whether the sibling had autism, mental retardation, or was developing typically (McHale, Sloan, & Simeonsson, 1986). However, these researchers caution that siblings of children with disabilities gave varied responses. Some children had very positive things to say about their experiences with a brother or sister with autism or mental retardation, and others were quite negative. The siblings in the negative group often said they were worried about the future of the child with a disability, and they believed their parents favored that child. By contrast, children who viewed both parents and peers as responding positively to the child's disability and who had a good factual understanding of the disability tended to have a more positive relationship with their brother or sister. The focus on this book is on improving your child's understanding of autism and ability to relate to her sibling with autism.

Another team of researchers compared siblings of children with autism to siblings of children with Down syndrome and of typically developing children (Rodrique, Geffken, & Morgan, 1993). They found that the parents of the children with autism reported more concerns about what psychologists call internalizing and externalizing symptoms. Internalizing symptoms are those we experience inwardly, such as depression and anxiety, while externalizing symptoms are turned outside of ourselves in behaviors such as aggression, defiance, or  running away. Although both of these kinds of problems were more frequent in the children who had siblings with autism, the young people as a group still fell within the normal range of behavior. In addition, on the positive side, the siblings of the children with autism did not differ from the other two groups in their self-esteem.* The findings of more emotional and behavior problems in the siblings of children with autism support the idea that it is harder to be the sibling of a child with autism than of a child with another disability, and heighten the importance for parents of being alert to their children's struggles.

Yet another recent study compared the relationship among siblings of children with autism with those whose siblings had Down syndrome or no known disabilities (Kaminsky & Dewey, 2001). They found that the siblings of children with autism, who ranged from eight to eighteen years of age, experienced less sibling intimacy, positive social interaction, and nurturance than the other groups of children did. This finding is consistent with what we know about autism, in that children with this disability would usually have difficulty showing empathy, helpfulness, and warmth toward their brother or sister. Interestingly, this study also found that the siblings of the children with autism or Down syndrome described a greater admiration for their brother or sister and fewer feelings of competition than did the siblings of typically developing children. This reflects the positive feelings these children have about their brother or sister and their compassion for the challenges these youngsters face.

These research studies are consistent with our own experiences working with siblings across the age spectrum. It appears that most children are resilient to the impact of their brother's or sister's special needs. Nonetheless, there *are* challenges involved in growing up in a family where a sibling has autism and the relationship *does* differ from that between typically developing children. The purpose of this book is to help the reader understand these potential issues and be able to minimize their impact.

Special Demands

Information Needs

Researchers Milton Seligman and Rosalyn Darling (1997) point to several areas where siblings of children with autism may need help learning to cope. One of these areas is the need for information. Parents may not communicate openly or effectively to children about the nature of autism. The lack of information leaves a big space in the child's mind to be filled by misinformation, fears, and fantasies. Children will create their own explanations, worry needlessly about whether they harmed their sibling, or imagine a future life for themselves or their sibling far bleaker than reality.

Young children in particular have a difficult time distinguishing wish from reality, and may become very confused about their sibling's disability. Although they hear the word "autism," they may not understand what it means. They may, for example, be afraid that they caused the autism by some misbehavior or angry thought, or that they can "catch" autism as they would a cold. To compound matters, as noted earlier in the case of Kevin and Mitch McGuire,[children may be afraid to ask questions or raise problems because they do not wish to upset their parents or because they are ashamed of their own feelings of anger, jealousy, or resentment.*Children growing up under these conditions may learn to conceal feelings, deny their emotions to themselves, and develop an inconsistency between feelings and actions.] For example, a child might be frightened, but rather than expressing his fear, he might act very boldly in a way that could place him in danger, or he might act as though he wanted no support or affection, when he actually wishes that his parents would recognize his sadness. These behaviors can intrude on their capacity as adults for intimacy and form a barrier to relationships with other people. Fortunately, it is usually possible for parents to recognize and address these childhood concerns.

Having difficulties understanding about autism can also diminish a child's feeling of being a unique and special person, entitled to lead a separate life.[Some children may overly identify with their sibling and feel responsible for his disability (Seligman & Darling, 1997). A lack of information may make it difficult for the typically developing child to have a clear sense of himself as a unique person, not an extension of his brother.] For example, a boy may be reluctant to go away to summer camp because his younger brother with autism cannot go as well. It may be hard for him to understand that he can have a separate, happy life apart from his brother. Over time, if he continues to have trouble separating himself from his brother, he may grow up to be an adult who cannot lay claim to the basic right to exist as a special, unique person. In order to establish healthy adult relationships, we need to experience the legitimacy of our own needs as well as others' needs. Again, a perceptive parent can often recognize the seeds of such a problem.

Chapter 2 will describe in depth how children think about autism. In Chapter 3 we will discuss what kinds of things you will want to tell your child about autism, and how you can convey that information according to the age of your child. This information may give your child a realistic sense of his sibling's special needs and why there are differences in how the two of them are treated.

Play Skills

Children with autism usually do not meet their siblings' expectations as playmates. As we noted earlier in this chapter, at the age of three or four, a typically developing child begins to be a real companion to brothers or sisters. For example, he may be the "baby" in a pretend family or enjoy roughhousing in the backyard. By contrast, a sibling with autism of that same age may demonstrate a number of troubling autistic behaviors and be a difficult, if not impossible, playmate. He may destroy toys, be aggressive, or have severe tantrums when approached by a sibling.

When a typically developing sibling is consistently rejected, he may give up trying to play with his sibling. In Chapter 6, we will discuss how you can teach your children skills that may help them become playmates with their brother or sister with autism. This may help to strengthen the bond between your children.

Caretaking Responsibilities

Caretaking is another area that has been identified as a potential problem area for typically developing siblings (Seligman & Darling, 1997). Older children, especially older sisters of children who have both autism and mental retardation, spend more time in caretaking roles than other siblings do (McHale & V. Harris, 1992). For example, a sibling may help her brother with autism dress in the morning or supervise his play while parents prepare dinner. The more even distribution of care giving that usually happens when a younger child reaches eleven or twelve years of age typically does not occur in families where the younger child has autism. As a result, the older child may have a more difficult time achieving her adolescent independence unless parents are especially sensitive to her needs. Parents must be alert to the danger of allowing their adolescent child to be too good a helper, thereby interfering with her social development.]

These inequities of the caretaking relationship can affect younger siblings as well as older ones. [For younger siblings, the reversal of traditional roles can be especially perplexing.] For ex-

ample, a nine-year-old sister may find herself looking after a thirteen-year-old brother, in stark contrast to the typical age-appropriate roles she sees in other families. She may resent having to care for someone who is physically older and larger or be embarrassed to have her friends see her caring for him. She may also feel guilty about being younger and more competent than her big brother. In the normal course of events, older children care for younger ones, and children may be acutely aware of being different from their peers in this regard. The sense of being different can make a child feel angry, ashamed, embarrassed, sad, or defiant. She may avoid being with her brother, not want to have friends over to play when he is home, or perhaps join in when her friends tease him.

Helping take care of a sibling need not be harmful when carefully balanced with opportunities for other activities, [but excessive burdens can harm a child's development and a positive sibling bond.] The typically developing sibling is not an auxiliary parent of the sibling with autism and should not be expected to assume major responsibilities for that child. On the other hand, every child should contribute to the welfare of his family. The challenge is to find age-appropriate ways for children to make these contributions. Chapter 5 discusses how you can communicate effectively with your children about responsibilities and privileges and help your typically developing children understand that you love all your children equally, even though you must sometimes pay more attention to your child with autism. The chapter also discusses distribution of family responsibilities and opportunities.

Most of us feel angry from time to time. It is not surprising that siblings of children with autism must struggle with this emotion. Anger can arise if siblings are given excessive responsibilities for the child with special needs, if they feel their social life is limited, if they lose parental attention, and if there is a drain of family resources (Seligman & Darling, 1997). In the case of Kevin and Mitch McGuire, Kevin was ashamed of his jealous feelings, but he was also angry at his parents because they spent so much time caring for Mitch. A child who must spend most of his after-school hours caring for a sibling with autism, who feels he cannot bring his friends home because of his sister's tantrums, and who is always the loser in competition for parental attention may feel a great deal of anger. Chapter 5 will discuss how balancing the needs of family members is a difficult but essential art.

Looking on the Bright Side

It is important not to focus only on potential problems. There can be plenty of joy in a household that includes a child with a developmental disability. Your other children can take pride in the achievements of your child with autism, for example, sharing in the sense of achievement when he learns to speak, participates in the Special Olympics, rides a bike with other kids, or learns to play cooperatively. The siblings should, of course, also have many opportunities to celebrate their own achievements. A family that copes effectively can rejoice in the achievements of every member, feel closer to one another because they know that have dealt well with difficult circumstances, and know the special pleasure that comes from realizing one can handle life's many challenges.

Adults will often say that their experiences as a sibling of a child with a disability, whether autism, mental retardation, or a mobility disorder, taught them a patience and tolerance they might not otherwise have learned. Some may even pursue a career in a helping profession as a result of their experiences. Chapter 7 discusses the possible effects on vocational choices in more detail.

Adulthood

We noted earlier that sibling relationships typically endure across the lifespan. Under the best of conditions, this can mean the potential for intimate sharing with a beloved companion throughout one's life. However, when a sibling has autism, it also means enduring responsibilities for that brother or sister. As long as parents are alive, the sibling role in care generally remains modest, and most mothers express a wish to buffer the sibling from significant responsibility (Holmes & Carr, 1991). However, after the death or incapacitation of a parent, this pattern must shift. In some families, that may mean that an adult sibling takes his brother or sister with autism into his own home. For many families, it means that the individual with autism moves into a group home or supervised apartment and his adult sibling stays in touch and handles the various problems that arise.

These responsibilities may not be excessive or burdensome, and are often viewed as an act of love from one sibling to another. However, the continuing requirements of a brother or sister with autism can pose significant additional demands when combined with the adult sibling's needs to care for his own children, his aging parents, his marriage, and work responsibilities. In addition, adults who have siblings with autism have shared with us their sense of sadness when they could not seek solace from their brother or sister after a painful event such as the death of a parent. Instead, they had to bear the burden of their sorrow alone and respond to the on-going needs of their sibling as well.

For some siblings who failed to come to terms with their brother or sister with autism in childhood, adulthood offers new opportunities, as well as new demands. Some people may enter adulthood without having understood the full range of their feelings toward their sibling with autism, or without having come to terms with these emotions. The feelings of anger, jealousy, or sadness they failed to deal with fully in childhood may linger and influence their behavior in adulthood. For example, one woman we know entered therapy because she could not get over the anger she felt toward her brother with autism whenever he came to her home. She realized the anger had less to do with her brother's current behavior than with the expectations she had carried from her childhood. An otherwise warm and compassionate woman, she was perplexed by her lack of patience with her brother and wished to free herself from her anger. A brief course of individual therapy helped her to feel less angry and to establish a new understanding of herself, her parents, and her brother.

Adolescents or young adults looking forward to their own lives may feel considerable concern about future responsibilities they may have for caring for their sibling. A young adult may feel that she is expected to take care of her brother in her own home, and wonder if anyone would want to marry her under those conditions. She may wonder whether her own biological children would have autism and whether she should adopt instead. She may feel constrained from moving to another city because she feels responsible for her brother with autism.

The more parents can help their young adult children explore these feelings and concerns, the better it is likely to be for all involved. For example, if your teenaged daughter believes you expect her to bring her younger brother to live with her when you can no longer care for him, she may be very relieved to discover that you intend to help your son make the transition to a group home, and simply hope that she will look in on him from time to time. Chapter 4 focuses on communication skills that may help you explore these kinds of questions with your child and Chapter 7 looks in more depth at what it means to be the adult sibling of a person with autism.

Closing Comments

We have briefly examined the relationships between brothers and sisters, noting that some anger, competition, and resentment are normal in all relationships. Although the nature of sibling interaction changes over time, many people are fortunate enough to have an emotionally meaningful relationship with a sibling that will endure over time. For the brother or sister of a child with autism, creating a positive sibling bond may be more difficult than for other children. Children with autism are less likely to be nurturing, or even to interact playfully with their siblings. They also may require a great deal more caretaking than other children, and do not follow the usual developmental path to increased independence. Although most children learn to cope effectively with their sibling's special needs, there is a great deal parents can do to help them with the process of adjustment. We will discuss those opportunities in the remainder of the book.

Parents Speak

This evening was particularly painful for us. We moved our dinner location from our kitchen table to the dining room, in hopes that the hum of the refrigerator is the thing that sets Juan off each night. We have had other suspicions for a while now. This evening's dinner started on a more challenging note than usual. Juan began to cry and screech from the moment we sat down. We said, "Juan, you need to sit quiet so we can eat." We provided him with all the things he generally wants but cannot yet request verbally. Nothing worked.

Suddenly Juan's brother, Manuel, spoke up. "It's me, Dad. Every time he looks at me he cries." I couldn't bring myself to agree with him, but I know it's true. There are no words sufficient to explain how this breaks our hearts. There is no reason for Juan to be upset by his brother. His brother is a wonderful child. He has the gift of unwavering patience and love for his brother Juan. Far more than any nine-year-old I have ever met. He has been bitten and scratched and screamed at, yet he still tries to play with his brother. We must do something to identify the source of Juan's frustration.

My wife said to Manuel, "That's funny. Maybe it is you." As if we didn't already know. "Would you mind finishing dinner in the other room so we can see if Juan will calm down?" she asked. "Sure, Mom," said Manuel. Immediately, there was peace at the dinner table. How do we make this OK for Manuel? How do we mend his heart?

Having a sibling with autism has been very different for Sam and Martha. To some degree, I think the birth order and personality of siblings has an impact on what the relationship will be like. For example, Sam, being the older brother, has always seen Tommy as the baby. He has been understanding of

Tom's needs, including all the extra time we have needed to spend with him. When Sam was younger he would get angry at Tom for touching his toys or messing up his room. As he has matured, he has shown compassion beyond his years. At times I think it has made him a kinder, gentler person.

Martha has had a more difficult time adjusting to Tommy. She is four years younger and he seemed to strike out at her more often. She experienced many problems dealing with him and it took a long time to get to the point where we are now. She has a great love for him but at the same time a fear of him. Even though she knows he is older, she thinks of him as her younger sibling.

[Tommy has had a profound effect on his siblings and, like it or not, will probably to some extent shape who they are as adults.]

๑๑

Stan is seven and has autism. His older sister, Sally, is nine. I worry a lot about what it means to grow up with a little brother like Stan. I want her to be able to bring her friends home and I don't want her to be afraid of him. I know our home has to be a little different than other homes, and I don't know how that will affect her emotionally as she grows up.

๑๑

I think the thing that worries me most about Art is how he is going to feel about Jack as they grow up together. Here is Art, a little guy at age five, telling his big brother Jack, who is eleven, how to do things. I mean, what is he going to think about that as he gets older? Big brothers are supposed to take care of little guys, not the other way around. I'm concerned that it must be confusing to Art.

๑๑

Justin is such a terrific kid. Sometimes I think he is almost too good. He spends so much time with his sister, Allie, who has autism. He acts like it is his job to do everything for her. I don't want him to resent that someday—to feel like she stole his childhood. I appreciate his help, but I don't want him to overdo. I'm not sure how much help is too much.

2 | He Doesn't Know What Angels Are: Autism Viewed through Children's Eyes

The Schaefer Family

The Schaefers were a kind and generous family with two children, Suzette, age five, and Joseph, age ten. Joseph had autism. They took time out of their busy weekend activities to participate in a research study that I (BG) had designed to explore how siblings think about autism at different ages.

I met with Mrs. Schaefer first to find out how she expected her daughter to describe autism. She assured me that she spoke with Suzette often about her brother's autism and that she thought that Suzette might describe it as a learning problem. Mrs. Schaefer anticipated that Suzette might discuss that Joseph had a special teacher with special ways of teaching him. Mrs. Schaefer also guessed that Suzette might talk about how Joseph didn't play with her and how that upset her very much. Interviewing Suzette's mother was the first stage of my research and it made me curious to learn what Suzette herself would have to say.

Suzette and I went off to a different room of the house. I showed her the tape recorder and we talked about what I hoped I could do with the information from the study once it was done. Then, after Suzette seemed comfortable, we started the interview. What followed was a completely unanticipated view of her brother's disability. When I asked Suzette if she had ever heard the word autism before, she said that she had. When I asked her what autism was, Suzette sadly *explained that it meant that her brother "doesn't even know what angels are." Although I was a bit taken aback by this answer, I proceeded with the interview. "Is there anything else that you can tell me about autism?" Suzette thought about it for a moment and then responded, "Yes, the angels are going to help him anyway."*

Introduction

Many adults choose not to share information with their child about autism or some other subject because they feel it is too difficult for her to comprehend—only to later discover that she already has the information from another source and understands the matter perfectly. Other adults may choose to share a great deal of information with a child about a difficult topic only to discover that what their child heard resembles the droning sound of the adult voice on the old Charlie Brown cartoons! Most often, as in Suzette's case, what children grasp of our explanations probably falls somewhere in between the two extremes: they have heard something that we have said, and have reshaped it somewhat. Unfortunately, the concept that was formed may only faintly resemble the information that we thought was shared.

One possible culprit for this type of communication breakdown is a process called "cognitive development." This term refers to changes in our ability to think and acquire knowledge as we mature.

As the famous developmental psychologist Jean Piaget (1929) taught us, children filter information through a developmental lens. This lens limits the level of abstract and complex information that they can process based on their cognitive development. It also alters the importance of different types of information for them. What matters to us as adults may hold little interest for a child. Because parents and professionals may not understand how a child's developmental level affects her understanding, there is a risk that siblings may either miss facts or misconstrue them when we offer them information about autism.

Although the research looking specifically at a child's understanding of autism is limited, we do know a fair amount about how children learn to think about other topics. It is possible to infer from that how they think about autism. Based on this knowledge, there are things you can do to adapt the information you offer your child about autism to suit her developmental needs. We hope that the information shared in the rest of this chapter will help you find the words to best meet your child's needs.

Children's Understanding of Illness

Aside from the study mentioned in the vignette about the Schaefer family above, there have been few studies about how a child's knowledge of autism changes over time. The most closely related subject to have received the attention of researchers focuses on the development of a child's concept of illness. While a number of studies address this aspect of cognitive development in children in general, we know of only one study that focused specifically on siblings. In that research, scientists assessed the general cognitive maturity of children with and without diabetic siblings, and then measured their level of understanding of diabetes (Carandang, Folkins, Hines, & Steward, 1979).

Surprisingly, while siblings of healthy children typically understood illness-related information at a level consistent with their general cognitive development, siblings of children with diabetes actually demonstrated a lower level of reasoning about this topic. The authors of this study offered several possible explanations for this finding. [One possibility is that the tasks involved with managing the illness detract from time for the family to discuss it. Alternatively, families may deliberately avoid discussing diabetes with a sibling for fear of burdening her. Finally, as suggested by Piaget (1929), emotionally sensitive topics are sometimes more difficult to process cognitively than other topics. Other investigations of children's understanding of illness support this final notion. For example, in summarizing this area of research, two researchers noted a tendency across studies for children with illnesses to demonstrate a weaker understanding of what causes illness than did their healthy counterparts (Burbach and Petersen, 1986). This might be due to the emotional significance of the topic to these sick children.]

Because there is so little research looking specifically at siblings, studies on the development of illness-related concepts among children in general may be our best hope for understanding how a sibling might think about autism as she grows up. In order to fully understand this body of research, it will be helpful to first review some background information about what psychologists know about children's understanding of concepts more broadly.

A Piaget Primer: How Do Children Develop an Understanding of Concepts?

Most of what we know about how a child develops an understanding of a concept stems from the work of Jean Piaget, described above. Piaget (1929) noted that children develop in stages. In other words, they spend periods of time focusing on a certain type of developmental achievement before moving on to the next area of focus. With regard to the development of concepts, Piaget identified three broad stages:

1. the preoperational stage,
2. the concrete operational stage, and
3. the formal operational stage.

Preoperational Stage. A child's reasoning is *preoperational* until about seven years of age. [In this stage, children do not use logic to formulate their thoughts. Instead, they base their ideas directly on their own experience. Whatever a child has seen or heard about a topic defines the concept, and different experiences may not be tied together. Theoretical information that is shared with a child may not affect the concept formed.] For example, a child at this stage who lives with two parents and a grandmother may define a family as a Mommy, a Daddy, a child, and a Grandma, even though she may know other children whose families have a different make-up.

Concrete Operational Stage. Next, between the ages of seven and eleven, children enter the *concrete operational stage*. During this period, concepts continue to grow out of direct experiences, but varied experiences may be linked together by the emergence of logical thinking. In defining a family, the same child described above might now incorporate her observation that her best friend's family does not include a grandmother in the home and that her neighbor's father doesn't live with them. Although each experience of a family is different, she is aware that they are all illustrations of the same basic concept. She might offer these examples as possible components of a family.

Formal Operational Stage. Finally, at about twelve years of age, children enter the *formal operational stage* of reasoning. [They now think more like adults and have the ability to engage in abstract reasoning. They can consider hypothetical events and information that they have not directly perceived.] Continuing our example, the same child described above might define a family as a group of people who are related and live together. She would not be bound by her own experiences, but would instead base her reasoning on the theoretical notion of the essence of a family.

How Do Children Develop an Understanding of Illness?

Decades after Piaget published his influential work, two researchers named Roger Bibace and Mary Walsh (1979, 1980) applied this developmental framework specifically to children's evolving understanding of illness. They devised a method of interviewing children and coding responses so that the *structure* of the response or way of thinking about the illness (cognitive developmental level) could be distinguished from the *content* of the response (fact, belief, or misinformation about the illness). They asked children twelve questions about such illness-related concepts as health, colds, heart attacks, and germs (Bibace & Walsh (1979). For each concept, questions focused on what the illness was and how one developed it. Initial answers were followed by open ended probes such as, "Tell me more," or, "Anything else?" This continued until the child had no new information to contribute. Based on these interviews, the authors identified various stages and sub-stages in the developmental progression toward full, adult comprehension of health and illness.

[First, their research revealed that between approximately two and six years of age, children use "preoperational" reasoning in thinking about illness, implying that they rely on direct perception. That is, whatever a child this age has seen or heard will bear more weight than logic or explanation.] Within this phase, there are three subcategories of reasoning about illness:

1. **"incomprehension"**—where the child's answers are nonsensical or she does not answer. (For example: "The flu is like French fries. I love French fries! I eat them with ketchup. My mommy doesn't like ketchup....")

2. **"phenomenism"**—where the child focuses on one specific, concrete symptom or manifestation of the illness. (For example: "The flu is when your Mommy stays in her bedroom and you have to stay outside and let her sleep.")

3. **"contagion"**—where the child views illness and cure as almost magically transmitted from objects near a person. (For example: "The flu is what you get when you play with somebody who was just sick.")

Next, from approximately seven through ten years of age, children typically use "concrete operational" reasoning in thinking about illness. While maintaining their focus on observable events, their reasoning becomes less limited to personal experience and more logical. Within this phase, there are two subcategories of reasoning:

1. **"contamination"**—indicated by a belief that bad behavior or thoughts, in addition to germs, can lead to illness. Also, multiple symptoms are now considered at one time. (For example: "The flu is when you sneeze, and feel achy, and feel very sleepy. You can get it when you play out in the cold and forget to put your hat on like your Dad told you to.")

2. **"internalization"**—indicated by the belief that illnesses and cures come from inside the body, rather than outside of it. In this stage, the child focuses on the fact that the illness must somehow enter your body in order to make you sick. (For example: "You can get the flu when somebody sneezes on your food and their germs land on your

food and then you eat them.") A very young child might understand that if you are close to somebody with an illness, you can catch it—but they wouldn't really have an explanation of how that happens. In contrast, a child in this stage would focus on the fact that the illness had to get inside of the person somehow in order to make her ill.

Finally, children begin to develop "formal operational," or adult thought. They can now consider possible scenarios and use knowledge rather than immediate perception to reason. Within this stage of development, there are two sub-stages of reasoning:

1. **"physiological"**—where illness is seen as due to a malfunctioning or nonfunctioning body part, and the individual also becomes aware of gaps in her knowledge. (For example: "During the flu, germs attack the lining of your nose, throat, and chest causing them to produce too much mucus. I'm not sure how the germs cause your body to do that, though."

2. **"psycho-physiological"**—where the individual recognizes the influence of the mind on the body. (For example, "I probably caught the flu because my resistance was down from dealing with so much stress lately.")

A number of other researchers have found that these same broad stages of reasoning also occur in children's thinking about AIDS (Osborne, Kistner, & Helgemo, 1993), cancer (Schonfeld, Johnson, Perrin, O'Hare, & Cicchetti, 1993), and juvenile rheumatoid arthritis (Berry et al., 1993). This suggests that these findings may also be a useful guide for us in looking at the child's knowledge of autism.

Siblings' Understanding of Autism: The Glasberg Study

Because autism is a developmental disability rather than an illness, and is associated with less tangible physical symptoms than the flu or a cold, we need to know to what extent the developmental stages described by Bibace and Walsh apply to children's knowledge of autism. The research that I (BG) did was intended to look at this very question (Glasberg, 1998; 2000). The children who helped me were sixty-three siblings of children with autism or a related disorder who were interviewed using a modified version of Bibace and Walsh's (1979) interview. The children ranged in age from five to seventeen years and were from New Jersey, New York, and Pennsylvania. I was interested not only in what the children thought, but in what the parents believed their children might say, and so for each child, one parent was given the identical interview and asked to answer as if they were their typically developing child. Parent and child responses were then compared.

Each interview began with the question, "Have you ever heard the word 'autism'?'" If a parent indicated ahead of time that their child had a related diagnosis on the autism spectrum (i.e., PDD-NOS, Asperger's disorder, or fragile X syndrome) that label was used in place of autism throughout the interview. If a child said that she had never heard her sibling's diagnostic term, a follow-up question was asked based on information that had previously been provided by the parent, such as, "Why does your brother go to a different school than the other kids  who live around here?" or, "Why does your brother have teachers come over to the house?" The child's answer was then used in place of the diagnostic term for the rest of the interview. For example, instead of asking the sibling how people get autism, she might have been asked, "How do people get to have a hard time learning to talk?"

As in the work of Bibace and Walsh (1979), questions focused on what autism is and how one gets it. Open-ended probes continued until a child had no new information to add. In addition, certain content areas were specifically addressed by adding follow-up questions if the sibling did not spontaneously raise a given topic. For example, if a child did not mention the effect of autism on behavior or the possibility of catching autism, she was asked about these ideas. Also, because growing up with a sibling with autism can have such a profound impact on family life both during childhood and adulthood, a section assessing the sibling's understanding of the implications of autism was added. The interview questions are shown in Table 1.

Table 2-1 | Questions for Siblings

Have you ever heard of the word "autism"? Tell me about it.

How do people get autism?

You've told me a lot about autism. How does having autism make your sister's life different than it would be without autism?

When she grows up, how will autism make your sister's life different than it would have been without autism?

How does having a sister with autism make your life different than it would have been if she did not have autism?

When you grow up, will having a sister with autism make your life different than if you had a sister without autism?

The children were grouped by age into three categories:
1. five- and six-year-olds (typically in the "preoperational" stage of general cognitive development),
2. seven- through ten-year-olds (typically in the "concrete operational" stage of general cognitive development), and

3. eleven- through seventeen-year-olds (typically in the "formal operational" stage of general cognitive development).

This categorization allowed two questions to be addressed. First, do siblings acquire reasoning levels about autism according to the predicted sequence of stages of development? Next, do siblings acquire these stages at the age we would expect?

What Did They Talk About?

Although the primary focus of this study was to assess *how* children think about autism at different ages rather than *what* they think about autism at different ages, a brief examination of the content of their responses confirmed our suspicions that what parents share and what children grasp from an interaction may be quite different. The children we talked to often demonstrated either a lack of information or misinformation about autism. For example, approximately one out of every five children claimed that they had  never heard the word "autism." This included almost half of the five- through six-year-olds, about a fifth of seven- through ten-year-olds, and one of the eleven- through seventeen-year-olds. Because almost every one of the parents had predicted that their child would be familiar with this word, it is likely that the term had been mentioned by parents and forgotten by the child.

Similarly, siblings demonstrated a surprising degree of misinformation. Approximately a quarter of the children either thought that autism could be contagious, or were not sure whether or not it could be contagious. While almost all of the children in the oldest age group were aware that autism could not be "caught," only about half of the seven- through ten-year-olds and two-thirds of the five- through six-year-olds shared this knowledge. A question then arises as to whether these children believe that they might catch autism from their sibling. The following excerpt from an interview with an eight-year-old boy exemplifies the reasoning that children might use to explain why they haven't yet caught the disorder from their sibling. This boy had not been familiar with the term "autism," but instead described his brother as "wacky."

> **Interviewer:** Do you know if it is catching? If M. has something that makes him not able to talk and act "wacky" sometimes, can you catch it?
>
> **Sibling:** Yeah.
>
> **Interviewer:** You could? How would you catch it?
>
> **Sibling:** By staying too close to him.
>
> **Interviewer:** So if you're close to him for a long time, you could get "wacky" too?
>
> **Sibling:** Yeah.
>
> **Interviewer:** Do you know anybody that ever happened to?
>
> **Sibling:** Um, no.
>
> **Interviewer:** Is there any way that you can keep from getting "wacky" like that too?
>
> **Sibling:** Uh, by not staying too close to him.
>
> **Interviewer:** You stay close to him a lot, right?
>
> **Sibling:** Yeah.
>
> **Interviewer:** Do you worry about that sometimes, that you could catch it?
>
> **Sibling:** Mmmmm . . . no. 'Cause I'm always in school.
>
> **Interviewer:** Because of what?

Sibling: 'Cause I'm always in school and he comes home early before me.

Interviewer: So you're not close to him enough to catch it?

Sibling: No.

Interviewer: But if you were home all day with him, then you could catch it?

Sibling: Yeah.

This child's reasoning provides an excellent example of the detailed myths that a sibling might create when factual information was either not offered or not understood. However, a sibling might also hold a less detailed belief. Consider the following excerpt from an interview with a sibling who had just turned five years old:

Interviewer: Do you know if it's contagious? Can you catch it?

Sibling: Yes.

Interviewer: You can catch it? And what happens if you catch it?

Sibling: If you catch it that means that you're autism, and if you catch it that means that you're three years old and you like to be in that school.

Interviewer: Anything else?

Sibling: Um, no.

Interviewer: Can you do something to keep from catching it? Can you do something so that you can't get it?

Sibling: Yeah.

Interviewer: What can you do?

Sibling: You can stay away from it.

Interviewer: So, do you have to stay away from your sister so you don't catch it?

Sibling: Yeah.

Interviewer: Can she make somebody have it?

Sibling: Yeah.

Interviewer: But it's only if you get close to her or something?

Sibling: Yeah.

Interviewer: How come you guys didn't catch it?

Sibling: We didn't catch it because if we get close to her, it just didn't blow up on us.

Interviewer: So it could still happen?

Sibling: Yeah.

For both of the siblings described above, providing accurate, developmentally appropriate information may increase the amount of time that they spend with their brother or sister with autism. In turn, this may allow more opportunities for mutually reinforcing interactions. See the next chapter for suggestions about helping your children understand autism.

Changes across Developmental Stages

In attempting to learn how children think about autism, the most central questions we asked were, "What is autism?" and "How do you get it?" As might be predicted by their age, five- and six-year-old siblings typically responded to these questions demonstrating "pre-operational" reasoning that fell within the "phenomenism" sub-stage. This type of reasoning relies very heavily on what has been seen or heard and often involves a focus on one very concrete

and observable symptom. Most of the children who demonstrated this type of reasoning identified their sibling's language delay as the key symptom. The following definition of autism provided by a six-year-old girl illustrates a typical response to this question:

> **Interviewer:** The first question that I've got to ask you about is if you ever heard the word autism?
> **Sibling:** No.
> **Interviewer:** No, you never heard it. That's okay. Do you know why M. went to a different school?
> **Sibling:** Yes, I know the name of it.
> **Interviewer:** What's that?
> **Sibling:** Douglass School.
> **Interviewer:** That's right. Remember he used to have to go there, where I worked, right. And do you know why he had to go to that special school?
> **Sibling:** So he could learn to talk.
> **Interviewer:** Mmmm-hmmm. Did he need to learn anything else?
> **Sibling:** No.

To this young girl, autism simply means that you need help learning to talk. This one feature of the disability has taken on the meaning of the disability itself.

Based on chronological age, seven- through ten-year-olds were expected to demonstrate "concrete operational" reasoning, a more mature and logical way of thinking than would be expected of their younger counterparts. Nevertheless, despite their age, participants in this group continued to use "preoperational" reasoning in conceptualizing autism. They had progressed beyond the five- and six-year-old group only as far as the "contagion" sub-stage of "preoperational reasoning," which involves almost magical reasoning about illness transmission. The comments of the eight-year-old boy noted above who explained that he would catch autism from his brother if he spent more time at home and less time at school exemplify contagion-based reasoning. While this thought pattern might have been predicted for the youngest age group, we had expected more advanced responses for this middle group of children.

The developmental level of responses provided by the adolescent group provided the biggest surprise. While they were expected to be using adult reasoning in light of their chronological age, they remained in the same general developmental stage as both younger groups. Although the language and general content of their responses may have become more sophisticated, the developmental level framing the information was still "pre-operational." Consider the following excerpt from an interview with a thirteen-year-old girl. Like the six-year-old girl above, who boils down her brother's disability to not being able to talk, she was asked to define autism. Notice that although she uses more mature language than the six-year-old, the content of the answer really does not change:

> **Interviewer:** The first question that I have is have you ever heard the word autism?
> **Sibling:** Yes.
> **Interviewer:** Can you tell me a little bit about it?
> **Sibling:** It's a disability that makes problems with language, and it causes children to, like, say stuff over and over, so it's about their communication, like it's really hard for them.
> **Interviewer:** So, the way that you would say that autism makes kids act differently is their language, communication. Anything else?
> **Sibling:** It slows development.
> **Interviewer:** Okay, so you said it slows development? In what way?
> **Sibling:** It slows down, just like, language and how you learn to talk.

[In sum, although the children in the study achieved more sophisticated levels of reasoning about the definition and causes of autism as they got older, the average response from children in each of the three age groups in the study fell within the boundaries of the "preoperational" period of cognitive development. Children are expected to advance beyond this level by seven years of age.] This delayed acquisition of concepts relevant to autism echoes the findings of the  study of siblings of children with diabetes described above (Carandang et al., 1979). However, because in this study we have no comparison group of children with unaffected siblings, there is no way to be sure that this gap between expected and actual understanding is unique to siblings. Instead, this could be a byproduct of the fact that autism is associated with more abstract symptoms than most other illnesses and disorders.

It will take more research to find out whether the challenge for siblings lies in understanding the nonphysical nature of the symptoms of autism or some other factor. A lack of social skills may be much harder to understand than a broken leg or the flu. It is also important to remember that we are talking about the average or typical response. There were children, especially in the oldest age group, who showed a mature grasp of the nature of autism.

It is useful to remember that just because a child is capable of reasoning at a more advanced Piagetian stage does not necessarily mean that she has more accurate information to start with. Even siblings who are reasoning at or above the developmental level that would be predicted by their chronological age may hold misinformation or create their own autism myths. For example, in the following explanation provided by a six-year-old girl as to how her brother contracted autism, she utilizes "concrete operational" reasoning. This stage of reasoning actually exceeds what would be expected based on her chronological age. Nevertheless, the content of her response is rife with false beliefs.

"When they're born, anybody, each kid that is autistic, they keep falling, in their mom's stomach, and then they're born. All the doctors put something around their neck and that's what makes them autistic. It's like they're bad doctors. . . . By when they're born, they keep trying in the stomach, then when they're ready, and they want to come out, they get thrown around, and the doctors put a little something on their neck ... they didn't do it to me because I was just crying, and I was so quiet, I went like this (soft cry noise). Because he was crying (loud cry noise), they put that so he could be autistic. . . . I was talking but he can't because all of the doctors were so mean."

This girl was so convinced that her explanation of how her brother had developed autism was correct, that following the interview, she requested to play the audio-taped interview for her mother. Once that part of the tape had been played, the little girl exclaimed, "See, Mommy, I figured it out!"

Although some parents, like those of the girl described above, were surprised by the content of their child's responses, as a group parents were keenly aware of the type of reasoning framing their child's thoughts. Their descriptions of how their child might respond to the interview questions typically fell within the same developmental level as their child's actual answer; yet, the facts included in the answer might not match what parents had expected. In other words, parents may not have been sure exactly *what* their child was thinking about autism, but they knew *how* their child might think about it.

Thinking about the Implications of Autism

Siblings in the youngest age group, five- and six-year-olds, demonstrated "preoperational" reasoning in explaining the implications of autism. As predicted by their chronological age, they thought only in terms of their own, idiosyncratic observations and had not yet devised logical strategies to relate one observation to another. They also continued to focus predominantly on one symptom. The following excerpt taken from an interview with a five-year-old illustrates "preoperational" reasoning about the implications of autism:

> **Interviewer:** What kind of things could your brother do if he didn't have autism?
> **Sibling:** Know how to write with pencils the right way.
> **Interviewer:** Anything else?
> **Sibling:** How to write the whole letters of the alphabet.
> **Interviewer:** What else?
> **Sibling:** He can know how to write people with pencils.

Clearly, she was most struck by her brother's inability to write. This implication of the disability was her primary focus, and seems tied to her own unique experiences.

In contrast, seven- through ten-year-olds typically offered more logical descriptions of the implications of autism based on the linking of varied observations and experiences. This "concrete operational" reasoning is exactly what would be predicted for children in this group based on their chronological age. For example, an eight-year-old offered the following description of the impact of autism on her brother's life:

> *"He has to go to one of those schools where people have to help them, and he has to go to a whole different place—he has to go to the [rehabilitation hospital] and Easter Seals, and he has to go to the [learning center]. Sometimes we used to have his therapy, they would make him play on this scooter board. Ummm, he would ride it through the*

*hall, and he was very good when we would play "roll the
ball" with him. I would sit on one side and he would sit on
the other. He would just like bounce it a little bit over and
sometimes throw it. He rolls it sometimes. It's to make him
feel greater, and feel it all around his body."*

This young girl is still relying on actual experiences in developing
her concept of the impact of autism, yet she is now able to tie
separate events together within one larger category.

The oldest age group, eleven- through seventeen-year-olds,
typically demonstrated "formal operational" reasoning when
evaluating the implications of autism in a sibling. Children in this
age range not only reasoned logically about past and present
events, but also could evaluate the impact of autism on hypothetical situations that had not yet occurred. Compare the following response of a seventeen-year-old girl to the question of
how autism affects her brother's life to the above response from
the eight-year-old:

*"Um, I think it makes it different whereas he won't really
ever have like a normal life. He won't really like it if he
stayed the way he is, he won't get to go to kindergarten
or first grade. He won't, um, get to go to his high school
junior prom. He won't, like, get to go out with his friends.
He won't experience a normal life. He won't go out and
feel like what it feels like to do things with your friends,
excitement, different things, like what a book is, how you
can get excited driving—go out and do the regular world.
Just like normal things we get to do every day. And it will
always be difficult, because my parents have told me that
no matter what, T. will always have, will always be
autistic and will always have that struggle. Whereas, like,
somebody like me, things that I take for granted, like just
going, going off and doing something with my friends, or
like excitement, excitement over graduation—he won't
ever have that."*

This adolescent has taken her observations of her brother's current behaviors and experiences, and generalized from them to imagine possible and future scenarios. This sharply contrasts with the reasoning used by the younger sibling, whose thinking remains dependent upon her past experiences.

In contrast to how they described the definition and causes of autism, all three age groups performed within the expected developmental ranges when talking about the implications of autism. One possible explanation for this improved performance is the difference in the two topics. Siblings do not typically hear others describing autism, nor can they see or name a body part responsible for interpersonal relatedness. However, they experience the implications of autism every day. They see what other children can do and know what their sibling cannot do. They hear their parents apologizing that they cannot attend a soccer game because no one will watch their brother. They face their friends' questions and may have to make decisions about whether to have other children over to the house. The concrete, observable nature of this topic may make it easier for siblings of all ages to understand.

Interestingly, while the parents in the study accurately predicted their child's understanding of the definition and causes of autism, parents consistently overestimated their child's understanding of the implications of autism. They thought that even their young typically developing children might grasp the impact of their brother or sister's developmental disability on the future and on new situations that hadn't yet been experienced. In reality, this would be too challenging for many younger siblings. This finding is particularly striking because it means that on the one hand, parents knew that their children's understanding of the definition and causes of autism was at a less mature developmental level than would be expected based on their age. But on the other hand, parents expected that their children's understanding of the implications of autism would be more advanced than would be expected based on their children's age. Thus, the gap between parents' expectations for their children's development in these two areas is particularly wide.

What Do Your Children Think about Autism?

Many parents reading this chapter may begin to wonder about their own child's understanding of their brother or sister's autism. You may ask questions like, "Is he wondering why his sister goes to a different school?" or, "Has she created some far-out explanation of why he flaps his hands?" There is only one way to find out for sure: ask them! And don't be surprised if the answer that you get today differs from the answer that you get next week. That is why we recommend that parents create an open door policy for discussions about autism, starting at as young an age as possible.

Just as parents might translate other abstract concepts, such as feelings or religion, into the language of early childhood, so too should concepts related to autism be translated. Furthermore, it is best if this information sharing is ongoing.

While any conversation about the topic is better than none at all, try to steer away from the one-time sit-down discussion and explanation. Because of the developmental considerations described earlier in the chapter, having "the big talk" will probably lead to confusion. Mom and Dad might think the topic has been covered, but the sibling's changing ways of seeing the world will lead to a constantly changing point of emphasis and ever-evolving questions.

Instead, make autism as acceptable to discuss as what will be served for dinner. Try to jump in and offer brief concrete explanations of any unusual behaviors or treatments even before your child asks. Model your own confusion. For example, don't be afraid to say out loud that you wish you knew if your preschooler would ever attend the same school as your typically developing child but you just don't know. While you don't want to allow autism to become a constant topic permeating all discussions, you also want to ensure that your children have someplace to turn with questions and feelings.

If your family has shunned the topic of autism in the past, it may be tough to know how to suddenly introduce it. Consider

using the questions and interview procedure described in this
study along with these tips:

- *Hear your child out* through her whole explanation
  before correcting any errors.
- *Stay neutral,* regardless of what you hear—remember
  not to judge your child's answers.
- *Be sure to praise your child for sharing her feelings*
  with you and acknowledge that you understand
  where any misconceptions about autism may have
  come from.
- *Keep in mind that you want your child to feel comfortable* speaking with you again.
- *Be prepared for your child to share intense emotions
  ranging from sympathy to guilt to anger.* Again, be
  sure to remain neutral. Your demonstration that she
  is entitled to whatever feelings she has may prevent
  her from judging herself about these feelings. Keep in
  mind that as your child is provided with opportunities to communicate with you, her feelings are likely
  to grow more positive.
- *Consider the following example* of how a parent might
  get a conversation like this started: "I realize that
  we've never spent much time talking about Janie's
  disability. Since Janie is so important to both of us, I
  thought we should make sure that we learn about
  each other's thoughts and feelings about it. Do you
  know what her disability is called?"

What about Your Child with Autism?

Unfortunately, the reasoning of a child with autism *about*
autism remains unexplored. There is no research assessing this
aspect of development for children with autism. If you have a
higher functioning child with autism, however, you may be faced
with the challenge of explaining autism to her. You might wish to

 apply the results of the study discussed above, as well as the interviewing model, to understand the way that your child with autism thinks about her autism.

Follow the interviewing guidelines described above and use your child's responses to develop a guide for your explanations. If you need to first determine the level of your child's conceptual development before presenting an explanation, it's okay to take your time. That is, after you complete the interview, analyze your child's responses to see whether she's in the preoperational or concrete operational stage, and then develop an explanation geared to her reasoning level. For example, if she's still in the preoperational stage and just concerned about how autism is affecting her and her alone, you would just talk to her about her own symptoms. The provision of accurate information at an appropriate developmental level will definitely be worth the wait. Finally, as noted above in regard to siblings, be prepared for the possibility of intense feelings associated with this topic. Your child with autism will need your love and support as she develops an understanding of this difficult disability.

Closing Comments

Children process information differently at different ages. This holds true for siblings of children with autism struggling to understand their brother or sister's diagnosis just as it does for other children grappling with other concepts. These developmental influences may lead siblings to misconstrue information they hear or to create their own explanations for events in the absence of accurate information. To combat this, parents can engage in frequent and open conversations with their children, taking care to present information in a way that best matches their children's developmental level.

Because development is an ongoing process, the ways that your children process autism-related information will keep changing, as will the questions they ask. By creating an environment in which open dialogue about autism is ongoing, siblings will be more likely to share ideas, questions, and comments as they arise. The next two chapters provide in-depth information about how to go about creating such an environment, as well as how to provide siblings with developmentally appropriate information.

3 | Why Does He Do That? Explaining Autism to Children

The Jansen Family

Chris Jansen looked at his youngest son's tear-stained face, and jumped from his chair, kneeling in front of the boy to fold him in his arms. Drew was crying, his clothes were dusty, and his hand was scraped. "What is it, son? What happened?" At first Drew was sobbing too hard to answer, but in the comfort of his father's arms he gradually began to calm down and tell his story.

Earlier that Saturday morning Drew's mom had sent him to the barbershop two short blocks away, and on his way he had met some kids from school. He recognized them, but they were in the sixth grade and he was in the third grade, so he did not think they knew him. Then, one of the boys called out to him, "Hey Drew, what you doing?" Drew smiled, flattered to be noticed by the older boy, and said he was going to get his hair cut. Catching his arm, the boy told Drew to stop a minute, and then he began to ask him about his brother. "What's the matter with that dumb old brother of yours, anyhow? How come he always acts so weird?"

Drew became indignant. "Leave my brother out of this. He's OK and he never bothers you." The older boys laughed. "If you think he's OK, then you're pretty weird too!" Drew turned around and tried to push one of his tormentors away. The boys laughed again, pushed Drew in the dust, and walked away.

Drew began to choke with tears as the words flooded out to his father, "What's wrong with Mal? Why won't he talk? Maybe he just

*doesn't want to. The guys are right, Daddy. He acts so weird some-
times. I just want him to be a regular brother. I know you said Mal
has autism, but why does he have to be so weird? I stood up for him,
but I don't understand why he is that way." The words tumbled out
until, out of breath and angry-sad, Drew finally stopped.*

*Tears came to Chris Jansen's eyes as he listened to the story.
Poor little guy. What a tough time he was having. When Chris and
his wife, Alice, had moved to this neighborhood, they had worried
about how it would be for Drew to grow up as one of a handful of
African-American youngsters in a mostly white community. Thankfully, with the exception of a couple of unpleasant incidents, that
had not been a major issue. But, now instead of racism, there were
all the burdens of growing up with a brother with autism. With a
sense of deep sadness, Chris realized that just as he was helping
Drew learn how to deal with the racism he sometimes met in his
daily life, so too did he need to help him understand autism and
learn how to handle other people's reactions. It might not be fair for
Drew to have to carry these burdens, but they were his nonetheless,
and he would have to learn how to handle them.*

Introduction

Drew Jansen's encounter with intolerance for persons with
autism is not unique to him. Many of us have had similar experiences in which other people have revealed their offensive misun-
derstanding of autism. It might be a neighbor who yells at your
child for venturing into his yard, or a stranger in a supermarket
who criticizes you when your child has a tantrum, or an uncle who
suggests you should either leave your child home or not come to
his family picnics. These experiences may leave you angry, sad,
and frightened. Yet, however upsetting other people's behavior may
be, at least you understand the truth about your child. This makes
you less vulnerable to these verbal assaults than your children are.
Other children, just like adults, will sometimes respond to a person
with a disability out of fear, ignorance, or meanness. That kind of

experience can be painful for anyone in a family, but especially for children. It is one of life's brutal moments.

In his distress about his experience, Drew also revealed that he understood very little about what was wrong with his brother. For example, he wondered if Mal just did not want to talk. That kind of statement indicates how little Drew understood about autism. As we saw in Chapter 2, that lack of accurate information is not unusual for siblings of children with  autism. Drew's parents would have to help him understand what autism is, feel confident of his factual information, and handle the insults, intentional or accidental, that might come his brother's way. Prejudice on any grounds is wrong and it is always destructive, but it may be a little easier to bear and to fight against when a person feels self-confident and knowledgeable. Drew had no words to fight back against his tormentors, because he himself did not understand Mal. So, although he loyally tried to defend his brother, he was overwhelmed by his confusion.

Although many children will respond to another child's physical or mental disability with curiosity, kindness, or matter-of-fact acceptance, others may react with ignorance, fear, or even cruelty. For the sibling of a child with autism, these negative reactions can be one more painful demand in the process of growing up with a brother or sister who has special needs. As a parent, you cannot anticipate all of the problems that might arise in the world of childhood, nor can you protect your children from all of the unhappiness they will confront, but with some planning on your part you can help siblings understand autism and know how to cope with another child's curious or hurtful response.

Combating ignorance and educating others is an important skill for a sibling. However, it is even more important that he understand autism for his own emotional well-being. The sibling of a child with autism must know about the disorder. Ignorance about autism can breed fear, and fear can damage a child's sense of himself and his relationship with his brother or sister. For example, a brother might tease his sister with autism, as he would any other child, and then feel conscience-stricken over mistreating her. Similarly, he might feel guilty about jealous or angry reactions to his sister. He needs to know what autism is and to understand his responses to his sister's condition, so he will be at ease with himself and with her.

To help your children be well informed about autism, accept themselves and their sibling, and fend for themselves in the world of childhood, you must be able to discuss the disorder in a way that is meaningful to the child. Precisely how you do that will vary with your child's stage of development. Chapter 2 described the stages of children's cognitive development and the limits to their ability to comprehend abstract information when they are younger. This chapter addresses how to explain autism to children of different ages. We have taken a child's age into account as we discuss this because we know how central cognitive development is to the kinds of information you should share.

In your eagerness to inform your child, do not make the mistake of sharing too much at one time. For example, if your daughter asks why her brother repeats back what other people say to him rather than answering their questions, she will be more content with a brief answer about his echolalia (parroting of speech) than with an extended discussion of autism. You might say something like, "He repeats what I said because he does not know the answer to my question. When he gets older he will repeat less because he will know more words to answer with."

Offer information as questions arise, mention the topic of autism from time to time, but do not overdo the educating. Children usually want some specific information to address a problem that has arisen. Often they will signal that they are satisfied with your answer by changing the topic, asking if they are done, or telling you outright that they do not wish to hear anymore just now. Respect that. You have an entire childhood in which to help your child learn what he needs to know.

The Impact of Development on Children's Understanding of Autism

Parents have sometimes reported to us that they told their child about autism at a very early age and that their child understood. Indeed, at three or four years of age, a younger sibling might say, "My brother has autism." Many of the little ones interviewed in the Glasberg study described in Chapter 2 said they knew the word. This seeming understanding may create a false sense of security for parents who believe that they have established a family atmosphere in which there are no secrets, and that the children are fully informed about autism. It may then be puzzling when they discover that their children seem misinformed and confused about the disorder.

One mother told us that although the word autism had been used around her home since her daughter was born, she was surprised one day when the girl, then six years old, came to her and said, "Mommy, what is autism, really?" We saw this same perplexity in the case of Drew Jansen, who knew his brother had autism, but had little idea what the term meant.

Psychologists who study child development would not be surprised that a child could grow up with the word autism as a household term and still not understand what it is about. Children are able to use words well before they understand them, and a boy of three or four years who says that his sister has autism may mean no more by that than that she stares at lights or does not talk. The concept of autism is quite abstract and will not be fully understood by a child until a much older age. As a result, it is important to present the information you share with children in ways that are developmentally appropriate, and to repeat the information many times over the years, in increasingly mature and complex language, as the child grows up. These lessons about autism are to be taught many times.]

For the Young Child

Keeping Explanations Simple

Most parents understand the importance of adjusting information to a child's age when they offer sex education. The simple ideas we share with young children about "where babies come from" are quite different from the more complex information we offer an adolescent. Similarly, the very young child will only understand autism in relation to specific, concrete behaviors. The two-year-old is focused on questions of "what" and may endlessly ask for names of objects. For a child this age, autism is lining up all the toy cars in a row, or throwing cereal on the floor, or riding in a yellow school bus. Although you might use the word autism

 in a conversation with a child this young, he has no ability to understand the word. His world is focused on specific behaviors and he will respond to those behaviors, positive and negative, as they occur.

It is not uncommon for children with autism to have a tantrum, demonstrate stereotyped, repetitive (self-stimulatory) behaviors such as finger waving or light gazing, or be aggressive toward other people. These behaviors can be a source of distress for the entire family and especially for siblings. A little boy may be terrified of his sister's tantrums or aggression, both frightened for his own safety and perplexed by her behavior. Very young children in particular may be alarmed by what they rightly perceive to be their sibling's out-of-control behavior.

Explanations will be of relatively little use, but concrete intervention may help. [For example, if your son is frightened by his sister's tantrums, he must be comforted and reassured. Later, if he can be encouraged to play simple games like rolling a ball to his sister and if he enjoys the game, that will be good for both children. The fact that his sister has autism has no meaning to a two- or three-year-old.]

The typical four-year-old is filled with questions, ranging from why the sky is blue to why he has to go to bed. Parents know that these questions can sometimes go on in an endless chain. Child: "Why is the grass green?" Adult: "Because it looks so pretty." (Or, "God made it green." Or, "it has special green color in it.") Child: "Why does it look so pretty?" And so forth, sometimes for as long as our patience holds out! A four-year-old's curiosity seems endless. If he has a sister with autism, he may ask why she cannot talk. He will probably accept that her silence occurs because his sister has autism, but certainly will have no capacity to understand on a more abstract level what the concept of autism means. Indeed, he is likely to be quite content with the simplest possible explanation.

[Although the word autism might be used by a child of this age, he should not be expected to understand the term any more than if he were told that chlorophyll makes the grass green. So, answers to questions must be kept simple.] For example, you might say that his sister is crying because she is afraid, or she does not talk because she has not learned how, or she waves her hands because she is excited. These simple explanations are specific, factual, and concrete.

By the age of six or seven years, the young child will use "because" in his language and offer simple explanations of physical events. However, his explanations may be based on mistaken assumptions. For example, he may have two friends who are the same age, but assume one is older because she is taller.

Children of this age engage in a great deal of fantasy and magical thinking. This ability to pretend is both part of the wonder and part of the torment of childhood. For example, a child may begin to concoct stories about a sibling's autism. A boy might tell himself that his brother's autism came from getting sick, because once the boy heard someone refer to his brother's condition as a sickness. The next step in his childish logic might lead him to fear that if he gets sick, he too could "get autism." Similarly, a little girl who has been jealous and angry toward her baby brother may wish he would go live in another family. She might be guilt stricken when he is diagnosed with autism because her "bad thoughts" gave him autism.

Parents need to reassure children about these fears, just as we show them there are no monsters lurking in the closet or hiding under the bed. We need to correct their mistaken logic, giving them the simple facts they need, such as that they cannot catch autism as they might catch a cold. Although children may or may not voice these beliefs if you ask them directly, you can often frame your questions so that they do not seem probing or critical and that may help them express their opinions. For example, you might say something like, "I know a little girl who used to wonder if she could catch autism. Then, she asked her mommy about that and her mommy explained that you can't catch autism...."

When your child is six or seven years old, creating a book may be a helpful way to summarize for him what he knows about his brother's or sister's autism. You can have your child dictate the text and illustrate it with photos you take or with pictures cut out from a magazine. For example, seven-year-old Joe wrote a book with his parents entitled "Joe and Jack." It was about Joe and his brother Jack, who has autism. Joe cut out pictures from a magazine of children playing, and he asked his mother to write down the following words with one sentence under each picture: "Joe and Jack are brothers. Joe likes to play, but Jack doesn't know how to play. Jack has autism. That makes Joe sad because he wants to play ball with Jack. Mommy says maybe Jack can learn to play with Joe. Dad will teach Jack how to play ball with Joe. This is a true story. The End."

Dealing with Emotions

For very young children, parents can expect to deal with feelings of fear, anger, or jealousy. Children at this age need to be comforted when afraid, helped to regain their control when angry, and given enough attention to minimize jealous feelings. For example, if your child is frightened by the odd behaviors of his older sibling, reassure him that he is safe and physically remove him from the area if your child with autism is engaging in tantrums or aggressive behavior that might be harmful. If your child is angry because your child with autism has done something to upset him such as taking his toys or knocking over his blocks, help him find words to express his anger and then provide appropriate restitution. For ex-  ample, if his blocks were knocked over, Dad might offer to rebuild them, or help him find another attractive play activity.

Similarly, if one of your children is jealous of the child with autism, help him express these feelings and reassure him about how much you value him. For example, you could say, "I bet sometimes it makes you mad when I have to stop playing with you and jump up because your sister needs my help. I used to get mad when my mom would stop talking with me to go help your Uncle Mike. It's OK to get mad about that, but you can also remind yourself that I love you very much and I will always do my best to spend fun time with you." Remember too that feelings such as fear, anger, and jealousy are normal feelings of early childhood and would be present to some extent even if there were not a child with autism in the family.

Young children enjoy using dolls, hand puppets, or other toys to learn about autism or deal with their emotions about their brother or sister. Fantasy play is a primary means of expressing feelings in the early years, and parents can encourage children to voice a problem and reach solutions through play and story telling. For example, if your child is upset by the tantrums of his sister, he may find it helpful to use hand puppets to playact the events and see how they are resolved by the puppet who plays the parent role. Similarly, making up a story that has a solution to a troubling problem may help him resolve a difficulty. Sometimes a child will playact the same events many times until he has mastered the solution.

Chapter 4 discusses other ways to help your children learn to share their feelings.

Keeping Your Children Safe

If the tantrums of your child with autism are frightening or endangering a young sibling, provisions must be made for that child's safety. For example, if your child begins to tantrum in the presence of the sibling, take immediate steps to separate the children. You might calmly ask the typically developing sibling to leave the room, saying "Steve is having trouble controlling himself right now. I need to work with him. It will help me a lot if you will go into the living room and watch your video until he is calm." After the tantrum has ended, you should seek out the sibling, discuss what happened, and explore how he felt.

Parents should plan with a sibling what to do if a brother or sister with autism becomes aggressive or destructive while they are alone together. Tell your children that helping their brother learn to control his tantrums is a job for a grown up, not a child. This draws a clear boundary between the responsibilities of children and adults. For example, tell your children to walk away

and call Mom or Dad for help. After Dad has handled the immediate crisis of the tantrum, he should touch base with the siblings. Thus, he might say, "I'm glad you came to get me when
Brock started to throw your cars. I know how scary that can be.
Maybe it made you mad too. I'm sorry it happened to you. Your
mom and I will teach Brock how to play with cars instead of
throwing them. But, until he learns that, we will keep you safe."

If your child has been hurt by her brother with autism already,
you will have to do all you can to prevent that from happening again
and apologize to your daughter for what you cannot always do.
Perhaps you can assess your children's interactions and identify the
precursors that signal that your child with autism is about to become aggressive. [You should also arrange some very pleasurable
activities for the two children so that your daughter will not be afraid
to be with her brother.] If you cannot find a way to keep your child
safe, you should seek a professional consultation to deal with the
aggression. Serious aggression cannot be allowed to go unchecked,
and there are many effective ways to help a child learn to control
those inappropriate behaviors. A Board Certified Behavior Analyst,
a well-trained teacher, or other professional who has an in-depth
knowledge of applied behavior analysis could help you design a program to deal with problematic behavior.

Middle Childhood

In middle childhood, from about nine to twelve years of age,
children collect vast amounts of information and may be a store-
house of facts about autism. They can typically understand that it
is a problem of the brain, that it is not "catching," that their sibling needs special education services, and so forth. If their sibling
also has mental retardation they will understand that this is an
enduring problem. They can shed many of the misconceptions
they may have had as younger children and become increasingly
mature in their discussion of the disorder. Table 1 lists specific
types of information that children of this age and younger can
comprehend and benefit from learning.

Parents will want to watch for receptive moments to offer information. Although some children will ask questions, parents may also initiate the discussion. Examples of potentially fruitful times for talking would include times when your child with autism is making a transition such as starting a new school, after you receive a progress report from your child's teacher, or following a disruptive episode that has upset the sibling.

Encouraging Independence

In middle childhood, children are starting the process of separating from their family, and focusing more of their social and emotional world in their peer group. Although adolescence is still in the offing, the building blocks for greater independence are being put in place. Children of this age will be joining clubs, going to slumber parties, and finding best friends. This increased independence means they will spend less time at home, and they may have less interest in playing with a younger sibling or one who has autism. At the same time they are maturing socially and emotionally, they are also changing intellectually and are capable of a more complex understanding of autism.

Table 3-1 | Telling Your Child about Autism

In Early Childhood
- You can't catch autism.
- It is nobody's fault.
- He hasn't learned how to talk yet.
- I will keep you safe.

In Middle Childhood
- Autism happens before a person is born or is a tiny baby.
- It is a problem in the brain.
- It causes problems with talking, playing, understanding other people's feelings.
- People with autism can learn, but it takes a lot of work.
- If your brother is aggressive, it is my job to help him, not yours.
- You can help him by playing and by showing him how to do things.
- If your friends have questions, I can help you figure out what to say.

[This maturing understanding of autism has the potential to collide with their dawning interest in a wider social experience, because as they start to understand the disability and its impact, they may feel more obligated to take care of their sibling. As a parent, you should make sure that your child's concern for his sibling not keep him too closely tied to home. Children of this age need to be encouraged to pursue their many interests beyond the home and family. This exploration of the world's possibilities and discovery of their own skills and abilities makes this a potentially delightful stage of childhood.]

Helping Children Fit In

Their growing reliance on their peer group can also make children of middle childhood very vulnerable to the reactions of other children concerning their sibling with autism. Some children of this age may begin to turn away from their sibling with autism in an effort to fit in with their peers. This can be very disconcerting to parents, especially when it comes from a child who has previously been very loving. Understanding that the changes in attitude reflect a developmental process may enable parents to be more patient, while still helping siblings understand that rejecting the child with autism is not acceptable.

One father called us in distress when he discovered that his daughter was calling her brother with autism a "dummy" and laughing with her friends. His first impulse was to yell at her and take away privileges. But, as we talked about his daughter's efforts to become part of her peer group, he changed his approach. Understanding that his daughter's embarrassment and subsequent rejection of her brother were normal for her age made it easier for him to decide on an effective response.

Although conveying clearly his disapproval of his daughter's behavior, this father also encouraged her to think about what she was doing and why she was doing it. With his patient guidance, her "bad behavior" was turned into a lesson in growing up. He also discussed with her how she could respond to her friends. For example, he suggested that if they called her brother a "dummy" she might say, "You think he's a dummy because you don't know him. David has autism and so he can't talk well. He goes to a school where he's learning a lot of things. He is really good with puzzles and things." Her father also suggested that if they asked questions she did not know how to answer, she could tell them she would check with her parents and let them know. He was also very much aware of how easily young people are embarrassed in front of their friends and took pains only to correct her when they were alone.

Acknowledging You Are Human

Children of middle childhood also become increasingly aware of their parents as "flawed" persons who can make mistakes. This is the time in childhood when parents begin to lose their heroic stature and start to be recognized as the mortal beings they actually are. As a result, children may begin to be criti-

cal of their parents for many things including how they are dealing with the child with autism.

There is no harm in acknowledging to your children that
you do not have all the answers. In the case of autism, as in so
many of life's
questions, no
one knows all
the answers. It
is not essential
that your chil-
dren see you as
all-knowing.
To the contrary,
they need a re-
alistic sense of
you as a person

who is able to cope with a problem in spite of the difficulties you
face. This provides your growing child with a realistic model,
rather than a superhero whose achievements can never be equaled
by the youngster growing up.

As your absolute authority and wisdom decline, so too will
your power to provide comfort and reassurance to your children.
As discussed in Chapter 1, while children will still seek their parents for consolation, more of their emotional needs will start to
be met by their friends. This transition to adolescence may help
prepare parents and children for the more active process of separation that occurs in the teenage years.

Adolescence

It is not until adolescence that young people become intellectually capable of understanding autism as fully as adults do.
Your teenaged children should have access to as much information about autism as they wish, although it is important to remember that factual understanding and emotional acceptance
are different processes and that feelings can interfere with gain-

ing and using knowledge.] We have all had the experience of yearning for things that we know are not possible. For example, a young person may understand intellectually that his brother's autism is an enduring problem, but still be reluctant to accept that limit on an emotional basis. He will need his parents' support in accepting the full impact of his sibling's disability (see Chapter 4).

Clearly, the difficult challenge for parents at this age is not explaining autism. The young person has a mature ability to grasp fact and theory. However, as we noted in Chapter 2, feelings may get in the way of fully grasping what autism is all about. A prime challenge for parents is helping the teenager understand what autism means for himself, his family, and his brother or sister and dealing with the feelings that knowledge brings.

The adolescent who likes to read may find a book about autism in the family library and read it on his own. Perhaps he will write an essay for an English class about his sister with autism, and he may include some of his own feelings in his written work. It will differ from a paper he might have written a few years earlier, because it will be more than a listing of facts. Rather, it may include an appreciation of theories about the cause of autism or a thoughtful reflection on the emotional impact of autism on his own and his family's lives. With your help or from his own reading, he will be able to separate out the effects of autism and mental retardation, and see how each of these affects his brother's development.

Helping with Behavior Management

[With older children, especially adolescents, questions arise about their role in managing disruptive behavior. Our own view is that older siblings can play a role in a program that involves positive reinforcement for appropriate behavior or a very mild punishment such as saying "No" or withdrawing attention as a consequence for inappropriate behavior. However, most siblings will not be emotionally or physically able to use procedures such as physical restraint, should that be necessary. In addition, it is essential that people who do not know how to apply these procedures correctly or who might misuse them not try to use them.]

Some techniques are not easy for adults to do, and may be too much for a child to handle. It is much better to err on the side of caution than to place too much responsibility on a child.

Except under very unusual conditions, parents, not siblings, are responsible for disciplining children. This is true in every family, not only those that include a child with autism. However, if you leave your adolescent child in charge for brief periods—for example, while you go out to dinner—he needs to have the authority to manage his sibling. Depending on the age, skills, and self-confidence of your teenager, he may be able to manage episodes of aggressive behavior if these are mild or the sibling is quite young. However, a teenager should not be left alone in charge of an older, larger sibling who might pose a real danger. If such authority places too much of a demand on your teenager, you should hire a paid respite worker, member of the extended family, or sitter instead. A teacher or psychologist can play a useful role in helping parents think about these issues in relation to their children.

Questions about the Future

Adolescents have the capacity to reflect on the past and future and may begin to grapple with questions about their adult responsibility for their sibling with autism. Similarly, determining their chances of giving birth to a child with autism themselves may become an important issue for teenagers. Because these questions of adult responsibility and childbearing are so common among adolescents, parents will want to raise the topics and share information if their teenager is receptive. Questions about the transmission of autism may sometimes need to be answered by a genetic counselor who is familiar with autism and knows the current research on its genetic inheritance.

These personal concerns may be very difficult for your children to express because they do not want to upset you, or perhaps are ashamed of, or embarrassed by, the thoughts. They may well reveal more of their thoughts to their best friends than to you. This is a natural part of growing up. The increased desire for privacy does not mean your children have become inaccessible to you, but it does signal that you will have to be alert to their needs and recognize the times when communication is possible. Many parents tell us that relaxed, private times are the best opportunities to initiate this kind of conversation with a child. For example, a drive in the car, or a Sunday morning around the breakfast table, may offer opportunities to begin a discussion.

Continuing to Encourage Independence

Teenagers are able to understand the distress experienced by their parents and be attuned to emotional issues that might escape younger children. For example, a teenage son may see the flicker of pain in his father's eye when a younger sister with autism turns away from his greeting as he comes home from work. This can teach him something about his father's life. However, it could also make the continuing process of adolescent separation from the family more difficult, because the teenager may feel that he needs to remain close to home to meet his parents' emotional needs. For example, he might announce that he wants to attend a local community college rather than living two hours away at the state university. Or, after having dreamed from childhood of joining the Air Force, he might suddenly say that he is going to stay home and work in a local factory.

There are many reasons why young people might change their plans or stick too close to home, but if there is a sibling with autism, parents should be alert to that as a possible factor in decision-making. Openly discussing the issue and encouraging your children to develop their own lives, may allow them to pursue their dreams. How to set the stage for this discussion is described in Chapter 4.

If your teenager is unable to make his way toward an independent life because he feels too responsible for you and his sibling, you may want to consult with a psychologist or other therapist for help in teaching the entire family how to shift its patterns of interaction. Your teenager may also benefit from such help if

he appears disconnected from his sibling with autism and reflects his pain through rebellion or chronic anger. See Chapter 1 for information about the types of professionals who might be able to help your family.

Adulthood

We will discuss the needs of adult siblings in greater detail in Chapter 7, but will introduce the topic here so that you can appreciate the full developmental span of being a sibling of a child with autism.

The adult sibling of a person with autism may assume a variety of roles in relation to his parents and his sibling. Once grown, he will have the opportunity to understand the emotional experiences of his parents and may choose to support them in their plans for his brother with autism. This support can ease the concerns of aging parents about the future of their child with autism and may be a link that strengthens their emotional connection with their other child. Although most brothers and sisters will retain these links with their family, as we will discuss in Chapter 7, there are some who will elect not to have much contact with their sibling with autism, and as adults that becomes their own choice to make.

The adult sibling may gradually assume increased responsibility for overseeing the welfare of his brother or sister with autism. Taking on greater responsibility requires that he be fully informed about such things as behavior management, community resources, and medical needs of his sibling. It is important that he have the full benefit of his parents' experience so that he does not have to start at ground zero when he takes over his parents' role. Over the years, as his parents age and ultimately die, he may become his brother's legal guardian. For the higher functioning person with autism, this oversight may be more modest; nonetheless, even those people with autism who function quite independently may still benefit from a supportive hand from time to time.

In the normal course of events, all of your children will eventually have to cope with the unavoidable life tragedy of your own death. Getting through this time may be especially difficult for your typically developing children if they simultaneously need to deal with increased responsibility for your child with autism, as one of us (SLH) discovered in speaking with Ronald A., a middle-aged man who has an older sister with autism:

Ronald shared with me how his grief at the loss of his parents was intensified by the needs of his sister. Mr. A.'s parents both died within eighteen months of each other, creating a great deal of emotional and physical stress. Mr. A. had his own family to care for, including two children who were grieving the loss of beloved grandparents. He also had to respond to the medical crisis that preceded each parent's death, make the funeral arrangements, and settle his parents' estate. Each of these is a wrenching, difficult experience. What intensified the process for Mr. A. was that he also abruptly became responsible for overseeing the care of his sister. She lived in a group home in the town where her parents had resided and he had to decide whether she should remain there or move closer to him so he could provide closer supervision of her welfare. It hit him with full force that he was fully responsible for her and always would be. Thus, the normal anguish that accompanies the

death of a parent was compounded for Mr. A. by the
special needs of his sister.

Part of life's richness is our ever-growing capacity to comprehend the significance of what happens to us. This does not
mean the experiences are always positive. There can be a justi-
fied sense of burden and real sorrow attached to being the sibling of a person with autism. But there can also be a new understanding of how much love and support his parents gave *all*
their children. You may not be physically present in your child's
life when he achieves that level of understanding about autism
and about his relationship with his brother and with you, but
the gifts of love, support, and wisdom you shared with him across
the years of his childhood will endure and form the matrix of
his mature understanding.

Helping Your Child with Autism Understand Autism

It is often very useful and appropriate to help your child
with autism understand what his disorder is all about. People
with autism who have normal intellectual ability are aware of
the differences between themselves and other people, and without an explanation of their autism they may be quite puzzled and
upset by those differences. For example, your child may be upset
that his sister is learning to drive while he cannot learn do so, or
puzzled that she is so at ease with other people.

The same kinds of information that you provide to siblings
can also be used to help your child with autism understand himself
and his own challenges—so long as you provide it in a developmentally appropriate manner, as described above. Knowing that
he has autism may help him adopt some perspective on himself
and may motivate him to learn new ways to cope with social demands. However, he will still need considerable help from you in
processing what it means for him and a great deal of guidance in

learning adaptive ways to deal with the problems he confronts. How much information you share and when you disclose his diagnosis will hinge on your son's developmental readiness to grasp the knowledge. Our experience is that most young people with autism find knowing "what is wrong with them" to be very helpful.

Closing Comments

In sum, as we saw from the research literature in Chapter 2, and now more personally in Chapter 3, there is a vast differ-

ence between the five-year-old who announces, "My brother has autism" and the fifteen-year-old who does the same. What the young child and the adolescent mean conceptually and what they experience emotionally about the idea of autism will be markedly different. Part of effective parenting is recognizing these differences and making your explanations fit the developmental needs of the child. You may not always have the answers to your child's questions. When you do not, a good book such as *Children with Autism* by Michael Powers (Woodbine House, 2000) or a call to the local Autism Society of America chapter may give you the information you need.

Being prepared with age-appropriate information leads you to the next challenge: communicating effectively with your child.

You need to know both what to say and how to say it. Chapter 4 discusses some fundamentals of parent-child communication skills.

Parents Speak

Over the years, my children and I have discussed Donald's disabilities many times—not so much in clinical terms, but in terms of their feelings about him.

There are times we need to explain Donald's behavior to neighbors or friends and that can be difficult, especially for the children. Martha explains everything away by saying, "Donald is just handicapped." Sam will go into more detail to try to get the other person to understand Donald's difficulties. Rather than define autism, he describes Donald as the child he is.

୭ٯ

Today, when I stand back and take a hard look at Annie's understanding of Matt's autism, I realize it has been a gradual process for her. As early as age three, Annie questioned why Matt wouldn't answer her or play with her. I would explain to her that Matt was still "learning to talk" or still "learning to play." Then I would prompt from Matt some speech or play directed toward Annie.

As Annie grew closer to five years old, her questions regarding Matt increased and grew more complex ("Why does Matt need help talking?" and "Why can't he go to my school?"). I told her that Matt had difficulty learning to speak and doing certain things because of something called "autism." I explained to her that Matt was born with autism, as were other children in his school. Annie wanted to know if he would "always be like this." I answered her by saying I didn't know exactly what Matt would be like when he was older. I did know that we would continue to work very hard with him. I told her that together we had already helped Matt so much. I let her know how very proud I

*was of her. I knew sometimes it was difficult for her. Matt put a
lot of demands on my time, and there were times when she was
in uncomfortable situations because of his behaviors. I gave her
time to speak about those feelings.*

*Lastly, I reminded her that we were a family, and that
meant she was not alone. I told her that we were fortunate to
be able to talk to each other about everything, whenever we
needed to. Then I said, "I love you so very much," and she
repeated those words back to me and gave me her biggest hug.*

෨

Zack is only five and Jeff, who has autism, is seven. Zack asks
things like why Jeff won't play with him or why he won't talk. I
give him simple answers like, "He still has to learn how to talk."
I hope that is enough.

෨

We have gone through some hard times since my daughter
entered junior high school. She seems to be embarrassed by me,
her father, and her brother Jack. She doesn't want to be seen
with Jack, whose behavior can be quite disruptive. My husband
and I are thinking of some counseling for her.

෨

I remember when I was a senior in high school and we had to
do our senior term paper. I decided to write mine on what
causes autism. Although I had grown up with a sister who has
autism and watched my parents cope with her every day, I
never really understood what made her that way. So I wrote
this paper on what made people autistic. I couldn't believe
some of the stuff I read about how parents made their kids
that way and I got really upset. I knew my parents were too
great for that. Then I found this book in the library by a guy

named Bernard Rimland. It was all about how autism was probably caused by damage to the brain. That made a lot of sense to me. Remember, this was a lot of years ago, back in the late '60s, before all the great research that has been done.

Ellen is fifteen and goes to the regional high school. This year they had a class assignment in English to write about their personal hero. I was moved to tears when I read her essay. She had written about her younger brother, Seth, who is nine and has autism. She wrote about how hard he has struggled to learn to talk and how brave he seems to her, always trying to get beyond his autism.

4 | Let's Talk: Helping Children Share Their Thoughts and Feelings

The Martin Family

Rosemary Martin glanced around the kitchen table. Her eleven-year-old daughter, Kathy, smiled back, thirteen-year-old Rich looked up from the book he was reading, and twenty-year-old Joe sat quietly at the end of the table, carefully inspecting his hands. Rosemary nodded at her husband, Dan, and he smiled as he said, "OK, time to call this meeting of the Martin family to order. Looks like everyone is present and accounted for."

Rich put down his book, saying, "Yo, Dad, what's up?" Dan grinned at his younger boy, and began to explain why he and Rosemary had called this family meeting. They wanted to talk about plans for Joe, who would be graduating from school in June. When he was five, Joe had been diagnosed as having autism, and he had spent the past fifteen years in special education programs. Thanks to a lot of patient teaching at home and in school, Joe had made impressive progress. But, in spite of all he was able to learn, it was also clear that he would continue to need some special services throughout his life. His speech was still limited, he sometimes got very uncomfortable in unfamiliar situations, and he had a lot of difficulty interacting with other people. But, he was a neat, careful worker who knew how to use hand tools and office equipment. He had excellent self-care skills and was a big help at home. Joe also was good natured and easy to live with unless something really major happened to upset his routines. It was very important to Joe that he keep things in order.

Rosemary said she wanted the children to understand the plans they had for Joe, where he would live and where he would work. Graduation from school would mean changes in Joe's life and for everyone else, so everyone in the family should be aware of what was being planned and have an opportunity to share in the discussion. Rosemary and Dan had talked with Joe many times to help him understand that his school days would soon be at an end, and his teacher at school was doing the same. Their parents had also shared some of this with Kathy and Rich, as well, and told each of them that Joe would be moving to a group home, but they had not talked as a family about the future, and it was important for them to do so.

When Dan said that they had put Joe's name on a waiting list for a group home in their community, Kathy got upset. She said she wanted Joe to live with her all her life, and she could not understand how her parents could think about sending him away. Dan gently reminded her that when most young people grow up, they leave their parents' home and find a place of their own. The fact that Joe had autism did not mean he could not be independent, just as Kathy and Rich would be when they got older. Dan said that he knew how much Kathy loved her brother, and that he hoped she would always spend time with him and make sure things were going OK for him. But he went on to say that when she grew up, Kathy would probably have her own husband and children to share her home. Joe would probably be happier in his own place as well, with friends to share activities, and a group home supervisor to advise him when he needed extra help or support.

Joe had been very quiet during most of this conversation, looking at his hands, and occasionally rocking gently for a few seconds. A couple of times he echoed, "Go to the group home" after his mother or father used the words, but he had not made any other comments. After Kathy had stopped crying and dried her eyes, he looked over at her and said, "Kathy's smiling."

When Kathy had recovered from her distress and the family was feeling more relaxed, Rosemary said that one of the things she and Dan wanted to do to celebrate Joe's graduation from school and increasing independence was to plan a family event. They wondered what the children would like to do to celebrate Joe's graduation. Rich laughed and said, "How about a trip around the world?" Kathy, who had volunteered to be secretary for their brainstorming session, wrote that down and then volunteered an idea of her own, "I'd like to take a trip to Washington. Maybe we would see the president." Rich chimed in again, "Let's think about going skiing. We could go out west." Dan suggested a trip to one of the islands to go scuba diving, and Rosemary responded that that would be great as long as they had horseback riding too. When Dan asked Joe what he would like to do, he replied, "Go camp." Kathy said, "Yeah, Dad, let's go camping in the mountains like we did last summer."

After a few more minutes of generating ideas, Dan suggested they had a good list of possibilities, and now they could go back and see which one would work best. After more discussion, they all agreed that since it was Joe's graduation he should have the biggest voice in what they did, and so they decided to go camping. Finally, Dan commented that it been a long meeting and it was nearly time to wrap it up. "Just to remind you, first we talked about where Joe will be living and working next year. He is on a waiting list for a group home and should be able to move there within six to nine months. I'll give them a call and see if we can all stop by for a visit sometime soon so you kids can have a look at it. Joe is also going to start in a job training program after he graduates from school. But, we also agreed that as soon as he graduates we are going to have a family celebration and spend a week camping."

As they were about to leave the table, Kathy got teary eyed again. "Mom, are you sure we will be able to see Joe after he moves to the new place?" Rosemary gave her a hug and assured her that Joe would always be her big brother. He would visit them on weekends and they would go to see him in his new home. There would be family vacations, holidays, and many times to visit.

Introduction

Good communication is vital to a happy family. Parents and children need to be able to tell one another what they are thinking and feeling. They also need to be able to sit down together to discuss problems and agree on solutions that meet the needs of the entire family. This does not mean that everyone will be completely

satisfied with the outcome. A lot of compromise is sometimes needed in family problem solving, and sometimes parents must make decisions that are not popular with children. Not every child will respond to her parents' reassurance as well as Kathy Martin did when she became upset about Joe going into the group home. However, open, honest communication can increase the likelihood that everyone will feel that his or her opinion was heard.

Part of effective parenting is creating an atmosphere where that kind of communication is possible. That means teaching children the skills that lead to the open exchange of ideas and creating situations where they can practice these skills. Children who learn from their parents how to communicate well with the people they love will find that those skills hold them in good stead all of their lives. Not only will they be happier with the family of their childhood, they should also be able to carry these same skills into their adulthood and pass them on to their own children.

Most of the time, family talks about autism or any other topic of concern to parents and children will occur informally, during the course of the day's routine. Sometimes, as we just saw in the case of the Martin family, parents may call for a family meeting to give the entire family a chance to hear important information and share in decision making. Dan and Rosemary Martin were confronted by a major event in the life of their oldest boy, Joe. Joe was graduating from school in a few months and his parents needed to make plans for the next step in his life. Although they had thought about this event for many years and had started planning in Joe's early adolescence, as the time grew close they had to take concrete action to make arrangements for their son. Ideally, the Martins might have talked earlier as a family about the options for Joe and explored the idea of a group home more fully. But this was an emotionally laden process and Dan and Rosemary had to prepare themselves first.

There were many painful moments in planning for Joe's future. Knowing that he was about to turn twenty-one was a powerful symbol for Rosemary and Dan. They felt a renewed sense of sadness when they thought about what a twenty-first birthday meant for other young men who would be graduating from college, launching a career, and perhaps getting married. None of these pleasures would ever be Joe's. However, they were also proud of Joe's achievements and wanted to celebrate his manhood with him. They knew how hard he had worked to gain his education and to learn to manage the effects of his autism. After they had shared their feelings, happy and sad, with one another, and made the decisions they knew had to make as Joe's parents, they felt ready to include their children in some of the decision making.

The Martins knew that their other children would feel some distress over the idea of Joe's move to a group home. However, as his parents, they believed it was the best plan for Joe and for them. They were committed to the idea, but wanted the children to understand what they were doing. They also wanted the children to feel that Joe was entering adulthood, an event to celebrate, and therefore wanted the whole family to join in planning the celebration.

Later in the chapter we will discuss some of the procedures the Martins followed to make their family meeting an effective one. Before we do that, we are going to consider some of the obstacles that make communication between parents and children difficult, and how you can create an atmosphere that makes it easier to communicate. Family communication when there is a child with autism is made additionally complex because of such factors as time demands, behavior management difficulties, and sibling issues that arise. Each family establishes its own style, its own customs, and its own rituals, but knowing some of the pitfalls and possibilities of how families communicate may give you ideas you can adapt to your own situation.

Creating an Atmosphere for Communication

Most of us value those relationships we have had over the years with other people who seemed able to look into our hearts. These were people who listened closely to us, understood our words, encouraged us to discover who we were, and sometimes helped us understand ourselves a bit better. We flourish in those relationships, growing more open, sharing our feelings, and coming to know ourselves better. Good parents do this kind of supportive listening; so do good friends and good psychotherapists. Love alone is not enough to accomplish that goal. Loving your child is important to good communication, but there are other things you can do as well to help the sharing process.

Good listening skills are essential to creating an atmosphere where your child will feel able to reveal personal thoughts and feelings to you. In the following pages, we will consider both some of the barriers that might make it harder for parents and children to communicate about autism, and some of the specific skills you could use to help your child feel more at ease in sharing experiences and in communicating with her brother or sister. People who use these skills tell us they are helpful not only in talking to their children, but also to their spouse, their friends, and their co-workers.

Barriers to Communication

Although most parents would like to communicate effectively with their children about a sibling's autism, there may be barriers that make this sharing difficult. One barrier is the emotional reactions parents may feel about the impact of autism on the life of a cherished child. It is quite common for parents to feel such emotions as deep sadness, loss, or anger about their child's autism. These feelings are a normal response to the tragic effect of autism on a child's development.

Parents may fear revealing negative feelings to their children because they are ashamed of the feelings, think they are abnormal, or because they do not wish to burden the children with their emo-tions. Unfortunately, it is difficult to keep our feelings secret, especially from family members who share our home and see our moods on a daily basis. Although a child may not understand the reason Dad is sad or Mom is angry, she is very likely to pick up on the feelings. She will notice the sadness in your face, the edge of anger in your voice, your lack of pleasure in the small things, or your preoccupation with your own thoughts.

Most of us cannot conceal the clues to our real feelings. Your child will notice these changes in you and react to them. If she has no other explanation, she may attribute your distress to something she did, and she may begin to blame herself for some imagined offense. Every child does little things that make her feel guilty. These are often minor infractions that are unimportant to us as adults. However, in her mind these childish misbehaviors can loom large and be magnified into the reason that you are upset. As we saw in Chapters 2 and 3, sometimes a child can frighten herself with the things she imagines.

Clearly, parents do not wish to burden children with the full intensity of their feelings of grief, anxiety, or disappointment about a sibling's autism. Such feelings are best shared between husband and wife as Dan and Rosemary Martin did, or with friends, minister, priest, or rabbi, or a professional therapist. However, children can understand that parents feel a range of emotions. They can accept that sadness, anger, or regret may be among the many reactions, along with love, concern, and other positive feelings, that parents experience in relation to a child.

If you label your own emotions, and explain that they are linked to feelings of concern for your child with autism, but do not diminish your love for that child or for the other children, this may help to ease siblings' concerns about your emotional state. At the very least, your child will know she is not the cause of your distress, and she can realistically label your feelings as due to other events in your life. You can share "good" feelings as well as "bad," both when your child comments on your behavior and when she does not. Very young children need simple labels like "happy," "sad," or "mad," while older children can deal with more complex feelings of frustration, sorrow, or exhilaration. Although labeling these feelings is important, parents are also entitled to the privacy of their own feelings, and you should respect your own needs just as you do your child's. Share what you are able, but do not feel obligated to share what you need to keep private.

Here is an example of appropriate sharing of adult feelings:
Mrs. S. had been preoccupied with finding a school for her young son with autism, but realized that she had not paid much attention to her older daughter. She made it a point to find a time for special sharing, by taking her daughter to lunch on Saturday afternoon while her husband spent time with their son. During their lunch she said, "I feel like I've really missed spending time with you the last few weeks. I've been so worried about finding

the right school for Donnie that I could not be with you as much as I like to. So, I really wanted to be sure we had some special time together today. How has it been going for you?" Her daughter basked in the warmth of special attention and both of them enjoyed their time together.

In addition to wishing to protect children from their adult feelings, parents may also hope to spare children from having to confront the painful reality of their sibling's disability. This protection may, however, only heighten the mystery of the child's autism. As we discussed in Chapters 2 and 3, the explanations siblings invent for their brother's or sister's behavior can be far more frightening than the realities of the disorder. It is therefore important that you provide age-appropriate explanations and ensure that siblings have facts, not fantasy, about autism. This information may also help your children understand why their sibling with autism needs extra parental attention, and ease some of the jealous or resentful feelings that almost inevitably follow when one child sees her parent paying more attention to another child. Once again, the truth is healthier than a fantasy your child might create to explain why you spend more time with her brother with autism than you do with her.

Between Husband and Wife

Good communication in a family has to happen between husband and wife as well as between parent and child. What happens between parents matters not only to those two adults, but to the children as well, as illustrated by the following story:

A father confided in us that he was struggling with feelings of anger and grief about his young son's autism. He felt unable to share these feelings with his wife, because he knew how upset she was over their son's diagnosis. As her husband, he believed he needed to be strong and protect her from his sorrow. Ironically, a few weeks before, his wife had shared how upset she was by her husband's apparent lack of distress about their son. She could not understand why he did not seem to care very much about the boy's problems. She felt all alone with her sadness.

In this case, a bit of encouragement to the father to share some of his feelings with his wife allowed them both to feel better. He realized that his wife respected his feelings of sorrow, and she discovered she was not alone in her pain. This improvement in their own communication allowed them both to be more open with their eight-year-old daughter, who was going through her own process of adjustment to her brother's disability. None of us stands alone in a family.

Those principals of communication are not just for husband and wife. Any two or more adults who are raising a child need to be able to talk to one another. If you are a grandparent who is helping your adult child raise her family, or an uncle who has stepped in to be a "father" in a family who has lost its own father, you will also need to become adept at this kind of communication.

Learning to communicate with a spouse or partner takes practice, effort, and trust. Some general principles to follow are outlined in the section on "Skills for Communicating" below.

Some couples do very well at communicating, but others may need outside help to get the process going. Consulting a professional therapist or religious advisor with counseling skills is a wise course of action if a marriage or other close childrearing relationship is especially unhappy.

Between Children

When one child has autism, the verbal communication between siblings may be very limited. This will be especially true if your child with autism also has mental retardation, as we saw in the case of Joe Martin that opened this chapter. Joe lacked much of the vocabulary and sentence structure, as well as the ability to understand, needed to take part in the interpersonal complexities of conversation. Under these conditions, words will be of limited value, and the child with autism will communicate mainly through behavior. If your child with autism does not have mental retardation, she might have a full vocabulary and be able to generate grammatically correct sentences, but still not be able to understand and express emotional reactions. Thus, regardless of the intellectual functioning level of your child with autism, the communication between your children will be improved if you can be sensitive to the frustration of

your typically developing child in trying to understand the child with autism, and can provide the necessary support to help the process move forward.

If your child with autism is not yet speaking, but is learning an alternative form of communication such as  sign language or a Picture Exchange Communication System (Bondy & Frost, 2001), it is important that her siblings learn how to use this system as well. They may want to suggest teaching your child some signs or pictures that are important in their play together and that would make it easier for them to communicate with her. The rudiments of these systems are easy enough for even a young child to master.

When your children are young, you will have to actively structure much of their communication. You can attempt to translate the behavior of the child with autism for her sister. For example, "She ignores you because she doesn't know how to play," or "Tantrums are the only way Julia knows how to say 'no.'" As she gets older, your typically developing child will learn to "read" her sister's behavior and to interpret her language. A higher functioning child with autism may become quite effective at conversing about factual matters, but be more limited in sharing feelings. Siblings should still be encouraged to express their feelings, both to the child with autism and to you.

Over time, your child with autism may become more aware of other people's feelings, and siblings can help with that learning. You can role play with your children how to respond if their sibling with autism does something that is upsetting. For example, your daughter could learn to say, "I feel angry now. I spent two days building that model and now you've broken it." If she can say that calmly and clearly, it may give her sister the feedback she needs to understand what she did. You can also work with your child with autism to teach her how to understand what other people might be feeling and how to apologize when she has upset others. The book *Reaching Out, Joining In* (Weiss & Harris, 2001) discusses how to help children with autism learn these perspective-taking skills.

Your child with autism will have great difficulty understanding her sibling. As a result, she may fail to follow instructions, not recognize that her behavior is upsetting, and largely ignore her sibling. This ignoring, or even active avoidance, can be perplexing and very upsetting to a sibling who yearns for a playmate. Both of your children will need your help in getting beyond these barriers. Chapter 6 discusses some specific things you can do to help your children establish communication through play.

Skills for Communicating

Open communication is important in every family, regardless of whether there is a child with autism or not. Some parents had more opportunity to learn good communication skills in their own childhood, while others may have grown up in families that did not talk much about feelings and concerns. If you already know how to let the communication flow between you and your children, you are that much farther ahead. But if you grew up without good models of communication, you can still learn these skills and pass them on as a gift to your children. The most basic skill to effective communication between parent and child is good listening. That is more difficult than it may seem, because most of the time when we have a conversation we are only half listening to the other person. We may be devoting the rest of our attention to scrambling ahead in the discussion to think about what we will say next, or how to solve the other person's problem.

Although teaching your child how to solve problems is important, many times simply hearing her out is more important. You may have found in your own experience that as you talk about your problems with a good listener, often you will come up with your own solution. Being able to "own" the solution to our problems is usually more satisfying that having someone else solve our problems. As a result, listening should usually take precedence over problem solving. For example, your child might come to you concerned because she wants to invite a friend over and wonders how that child will feel about her brother with autism. Your first response should be to give her a chance to talk it out while you listen carefully to her. If your daughter cannot figure out her own answers, or if the two of you need to arrive at a joint solution, that can wait until you have talked through the problem. Don't rush to the end before you explore the middle. The first step in effective communication with your child is to learn how to listen well. This takes practice.

Listening does not always involve words. Sometimes children communicate with their behavior. Parents need to be attuned to what children do not say, as well as to what they do. Changes in behavior can be important. The chatty child who has grown silent, the cheerful child who seems sad, or the cooperative child who becomes defiant, each may be attempting to communicate. The child who seems to be in special need of attention, who is clinging and needy, or who avoids her parents and turns away from their affection may be saying without words that she is distressed.

Be attuned to your child's behavior as well as her words. If you find that she has become moody, sad, sullen, or teary, you will want to explore what is going on. Her nonverbal behavior is an invitation to you to talk with her. Younger children in particular may respond quite well if you can make a good intuitive guess about their concerns, but even older youngsters may be ready to share their feelings if asked lovingly.

Rule 1: The Right Place

One essential of good listening is to be certain the circumstances are right. Unless it is an emergency, it is best not to have an important discussion until you have the time and can focus on your child. But, if you cannot respond right away, you need to be sure to set a time for sharing. For example, if a child mentions a problem while you are hurrying to get everyone out the door and off to school, it may not be possible to stop for an extended conversation. But, you can pause briefly, make eye contact, perhaps touch your child, and say something like, "No time to talk now. Let's do it when you get home." (And then be sure you do that when she comes home!)

Similarly, if you wish to initiate a discussion with your child, you need to find a time that is going to be conducive to discussion. A child who is eager to go outside and play soccer with her friends will probably not be very receptive to an extended conversation that keeps her from her play. To minimize that kind of problem, you might plan a private time together, or, if it is an issue that involves the whole family, call a family meeting for the purpose of sharing your concern.

Rule 2: Feedback and Affirmation

Another aspect of effective communication is checking to be sure you understand what your child is saying and then letting her know you understand. That can be done by occasionally making comments such as, "I think I know how you feel" or "uh huh" or "That made you mad." If you are not certain what your child means, you might try saying something like, "I want to be sure I follow what you're saying. If I understand you, it makes you really sad when your brother can't play with you like other kids do."

The process of reflecting feelings and confirming that you are listening carefully can be very helpful in building an atmosphere in which your child feels that you truly wish to understand her. Sometimes repeating her feelings back to her may help her clarify to herself what she is feeling. We have probably all had the experience of realizing that things sound different when we say them out loud rather than just thinking them to ourselves.

It is important not to assume you know what another person means when she speaks. Try to listen closely, and if you do not know exactly what she means, ask her to help you understand. For example, sometimes we use words differently. One person's "angry" may be another's "boiling mad," and your friend's "happy" may be your "sky high." One mother kept using the word "tense" when I (SLH) would have said "angry." When I asked her what she meant by tense, the experience she described fit very closely what I would mean by "angry," although she focused more on her physical sensations of anger and I might have attended more to the angry thoughts. I would not have known for sure what she meant by "tense" if I had not asked her.

Rule 3: Being Open about Your Own Feelings

Communication is a two-way street. In addition to being a good listener, it is important to share your own feelings and thoughts. That means modeling for your child honesty of communication, and sharing information and feelings appropriate to her age. We need to be able to tell other people what we like about them as well as what bothers us about what they do. Some people find it easier to share loving feelings than angry ones, while others find it easier to voice anger than love. A healthy balance of communication is important. Children need to know they are loved and cherished; they also need to know what they do that troubles us. Sharing negative and positive emotions in a constructive way is a valuable parenting skill.

Often we express our distress about what a child is doing by speaking harshly or angrily. This is usually based on the assumption that the child knows what she is doing and wishes to upset us. Although that may sometimes be true, frequently a child does not know she is upsetting us unless we tell her so. In addition, children often do things without being aware of their effect. A very young child may say, "Don't be messy" at the same time she smears a puddle of milk on the table. Her words and thoughts do not always control her behavior. Even older children often fail to reflect before they act. A child may need constructive feedback about a behavior in order to change it. How-ever, when we vent strong anger rather than sharing more modulated feelings, it becomes hard for a child to hear us, and perhaps hard to make a change without losing face. As a result, it is best when our feedback is clear but not overwhelming to the child.

Consider this example of sharing negative feelings with a child: *Mr. R. is upset with his older son. The boy left his model-building equipment scattered in the living room when he went out to play, and his younger sister, who has autism, found the equipment and cut herself on a sharp edge. She then became very agitated and was hard to calm. Mr. R. is at a choice point for communication when he hears the back door close and knows his son has just returned home.*

Let us examine two possible responses. In the first scenario, as his son walks in, Mr. R. gets up and yells at him, "You left your model-building equipment all over the place. Your sister cut herself, and then she had a tantrum and I had a terrible time getting her settled down. Why can't you be more responsible?" That may be an honest sharing of feelings, but it is almost certain to leave everyone more upset without solving the problem.

In the alternative scenario, Mr. R. says as the boy walks in, "Son, we have a problem we need to solve. I know sometimes

you get so excited that you forget to put your things away before you go outside to be with your friends. It's tough to remember to be neat when your friends suddenly come over. But, it makes my day a lot harder when you leave your gear around and your sister hurts herself and has one of her tantrums. We need to figure out how you can learn to be more careful with your things." In this second scene the father shares his sense of frustration, but makes the assumption that his son needs help learning to be neat, rather than that he is irresponsible.

The next step would be to problem solve with his son about their mutual problem. The problem solving would include agreeing on an appropriate set of consequences. For example, the father might offer to buy his son a new model kit if he keeps his equipment in a safe place for the next couple of weeks. However, if he is not careful with the gear, the equipment might be taken away for a couple of days.

Rule 4: Accepting the Other Person's Feelings

We may not always agree with one another, but it is important to respect the legitimacy of one another's feelings. If your daughter shares with you her anger about the time you spend with her brother, it is important to be open to her feelings and validate them as normal and understandable. If you get angry and defensive or guilt-ridden and apologetic when she shares these feelings, it will probably close off lines of communication. Do your best to put yourself in your child's shoes and listen respectfully to her feelings. For example, you can say that you might feel the same if you were in her spot or reflect to her that you understand how very upset she feels. If you can do that, it is likely that she will go on to share even more with you. The more fully you have heard your daughter's feelings, the more likely you are to be able to help her.

Acknowledging that feelings are legitimate does not mean that it is OK for a child to act on them. Your daughter has to learn to talk about what she feels rather than to vent the emotions directly. For example, she should tell you she is angry rather than tormenting her brother. She can also learn with your help to tell her brother in simple, clear words that she is angry at him, and as we noted earlier, he can learn how to apologize for his behavior. Even after he has apologized, she may feel that his punishment is not sufficient. You may have to talk with her about how you are helping her brother learn to behave, and that because of his autism sometimes the consequences for his behavior may be very different than she receives for hers.

Getting Outside Help

Although some children respond well to parents' efforts at communicating, some do not. If you are unable to reach your child in spite of your best efforts, or if your child's behaviors are especially troubling, you may want to consider the help of a professional therapist. For example, a sister who consistently shuns her brother with autism or who disobeys important family rules may need outside help. Similarly, a child who is chronically angry and repeatedly says such things as that she wishes her brother were dead or that he was in a mental hospital may need more help than you alone can give her. For some issues, a sibling support group led by a trained professional may be helpful in allowing older children to share with one another things they may be reluctant to share with their parents.

As we mentioned in Chapter 1, it is also important to re-member that some kinds of learning problems occur more often in siblings of children with autism than in the general popula-tion. It is possible that the problems your child is having at school or at home may reflect these learning difficulties. If you suspect your child has a learning problem or if a teacher has raised that question, you should get an assessment by a child psychologist, neurologist, or psychiatrist (see Chapter 1).

Family Conferences

Communication does not always happen one-on-one. As we saw in the case of the Martin family that opened this chapter, it can be helpful to bring the entire family together to share infor-mation or to problem solve when an issue comes up that may touch everyone's life. This can concern the child with autism or any other issue. A family meeting can be called by any member of the family, parent or child. Although Rosemary and Dan Martin had called the meeting discussed in the beginning of this chapter, any of the children were also welcome to request such a meeting.

These family meetings should be viewed as a special time. There should be family rules such as those shown in Table 1. At these meetings, parents can share with children important infor-mation, ask their opinions about impending family decisions, or jointly make plans for family events. People can also brainstorm about solutions to family problems (Forgatch & Patterson, 1989). This was the technique used by the Martin family to plan their celebration of Joe's graduation from school. As the first step, ev-eryone just tossed out ideas. It might be something as impossible as Rich's suggestion of a trip around the world, or as practical as Kathy's idea of a trip to Washington, DC.

After they had made up a list of possibilities, some wild and some practical, the Martin family discussed the list and finally decided that Joe's idea of going camping was the best of all. No-tice that the Martins all tried not to make fun of each other's

---

Table 4-1 | Rules for Family Meetings

---

1. The whole family should be present.

2. The television is turned off and the telephone answering machine is turned on.

3. No company.

4. Everyone who wants to talk gets a turn to talk.

5. Everyone listens while one person talks.

6. People should do their best to share their thoughts and feelings.

7. It is not fair to make fun of someone else's thoughts and feelings.

8. If the family cannot agree, parents have the final word.

---

ideas. Even when Rich mentioned the trip around the world, it was written down on the list as one possibility. People who do research on brainstorming tell us it is important not to judge the merits of any idea too soon or it will make it harder for people to feel free to make their contributions. The sorting out of possible and impossible solutions happens after the brainstorming is finished. Family brainstorming is a chance to let your imagination run loose for a while.

Closing Comments

In sum, communication is not a one-time event. It is an on-going process that shifts and changes with the ages of the children and needs of the family. Sometimes you will do a wonderful job of communicating, and sometimes you may feel disappointed that you did not listen as well as you might have or did not share as openly as you wish you could. That's OK. We all have our stronger and weaker moments. What matters is that the overall atmosphere in your family is one in which people are all working to understand one another's experiences and to solve problems jointly. Children can be very forgiving of mistakes when they know their parents are trying hard to do the right thing. Besides, there is not a parent in all of written history who did not make at least a few mistakes in child rearing!

Parents Speak

I firmly believe that if Tommy had been born without autism my children would have had a vastly different childhood. Be that as it may, the suggestion I have for other parents is to be there for them and talk to them openly about their feelings, whether bad or good, concerning the sibling with autism. We as parents have shared all of our trials and tribulations concerning Tommy with our other children. We have encouraged them to voice their opinions when they wanted to. This in turn has made them feel a very important part of Tommy's life and has helped to ease the stress in many situations.

I believe that as long as a family is open and honest with each other, they can get through almost any situation. Tommy is the prime topic of conversation in our home and no matter how the children are feeling about him that day, they express those feelings. Sometimes the problem isn't completely resolved, but at least they know we are there to listen and try to help whenever we can.

We went through a hard time with our oldest boy, Martin, a couple of years ago when he was thirteen. Martin had always been a sunny, cheerful boy who was helpful with his younger sister, Emma, who has autism. All of a sudden Martin went from being social, cheerful, and helpful to a sad boy who spent most of his time in his room. When I would ask him what was wrong, he would just get sullen and go to his room. My wife and I were at our wit's end.

Finally, one day I sat him down and told him we had to talk. I told him his sadness was tearing me apart and I needed to do something to help him. Very reluctantly he began to admit that he had heard my wife and me fighting recently about what to do for Emma, who was having some severe behavior problems. I realized that by trying to protect Martin, we had just left him with half truths about what was going on. When we sat down as a family and talked, it seemed to help him a lot. My wife and I also realized how much the situation was bothering us and that we had to do something to resolve it. We ended up going for some counseling with a psychologist, who helped us a lot.

I have had many problems with my older boy. He seems to have resented his sister since the day we brought her home. When we found out she had autism and needed a lot of special care, things went from bad to worse. Then, my husband left me a few years ago, and my son has just never gotten over that. I went to a psychologist, and my son and I had some family sessions together. That has helped some. I have learned to be more honest with him and he has expressed some of his feelings. I also learned how to set more limits for him, so he has to toe the line better now. All that helps, but it is not easy and some days I feel like I am climbing up a mountain too high to walk alone.

I grew up in a family where people didn't talk very much about their feelings. I promised myself it would be different in my own family, and it is. We talk to the kids a lot about what Christopher needs to cope with his autism and we share our feelings. I think it has made a big difference all around.

5 | The Balancing Act: Finding Time for Family, Work, and Yourself

The Gonzalez Family

Maria Gonzalez felt like she was doing 100 things at once. Pack the lunches, get the cereal on the table, find the baby's teddy so he would stop whining and tugging at her leg, call upstairs to remind her older girl to take the books for the school library drive. It was like a whirlwind every morning, getting the kids off to school and dropping the baby at her mother's before Maria drove herself to work. Carlos Sr. left early for work and missed this morning madness, but he got home before her, and was the one who met their son, C.J., when he got off the bus from school.

C.J. was nine years old and had been in special classes since he was three years old and first diagnosed with autism. Thank heavens for the school. C.J. was doing well, and now spent two hours every day in a regular class and the rest in a special education classroom. Next year they were going to try including him even more in a regular classroom. C.J. was bright and was doing fine academically, but his social skills and emotional control were still a problem. He needed a lot of support learning how to get along with other kids. Maria or Carlos had to spend time with him every night, helping him organize his work or recover from something that had upset him.

Driving to work through the freeway traffic, Maria wondered how they all managed as well as they did. Sometimes she felt as if she was stretched so thin she might snap. Three kids and a full-time job were just too much. Her oldest daughter, Natalia, was a *big help, but Maria worried that with C.J. needing so much extra help, and four-year-old Gus always under foot, she relied too much on Natalia. Natalia had been upset the night before because Maria could not come to a special program at the school Thursday night. There was a parent meeting at C.J.'s school, and Maria felt she must be there. Natalia had cried and protested that nothing she did was as important as what C.J. did. It made Maria feel terrible and she did not know what to do to help Natalia understand how much she loved her.*

It wasn't just her relationship with Natalia that worried her. She had so little time with her husband. Often by the time they fell in bed at night, they were both too tired to talk, much less to make love or even to cuddle and feel close to each other. Maria remembered with a sigh what a wonderful, tender man Carlos was, and she felt a loneliness for him.

The parking lot loomed ahead of her. Time to switch channels and concentrate on her job. She liked work and enjoyed the people she worked with. Sometimes the office felt like the only place where she had any private time at all. How wonderful to walk into her office, take a cup of coffee, close the door, and finally be surrounded by silence for a few minutes before the phone rang.

Introduction

Many of the demands faced by Maria Gonzalez are part of life in any family, regardless of whether there is a child with autism. Family life is a balancing act. Parents are often struggling to meet the needs of their children, their partner, and themselves. If both parents work, the demands are even more intense because all of the household chores must be addressed as well as the responsibilities from work. These stresses are inherent in family life as we know it in western culture. If there is a child with autism, the responsibilities can be further heightened by that child's special needs. These added needs of the child with autism can be so intense as to make it impossible for a woman to work outside the home, while the father may need to work more hours to make up for the income lost when his wife does not work (Alessandri, 1992).

As we saw in the episode that opened this chapter, Maria Gonzalez struggled to meet the many competing demands that faced her. Mother, wife, daughter, employee—each of these roles pressed on her, often at the same time. Each was valid, and each important. How to choose? Was it more important to go to parents' night at C.J.'s school or the performance at Natalia's school? What she really wanted to do was stay home and put her feet up for the evening!

Research suggests that mothers spend more time with a child with a disability than with a typically developing child (McHale & V. Harris, 1992). This difference in attention can lead to jealousy from other children in the family. It is probably not simply the amount of time spent with them that makes the most difference to other children in the family, but what they believe this difference means. If the typically developing children feel that their parents love the child with autism more than themselves, that will probably have a more negative impact than if they are able to understand the reason for the difference in attention. Once again this argues for the importance of good communication in the family.

Older children sometimes tell us that they know how hard it is for their mother and father to do everything that has to be done for a sibling with autism, and they  understand why that child gets more attention. However, even the most understanding of siblings is likely to view this difference in attention as very unfair at times. We saw this in the case of the Gonzalez family, when Natalia felt her mother's attention to C.J. was depriving her of the time she needed.

There are no perfect solutions to the demands on parents for time and resources. It is inevitable that you will have to make choices and sometimes one or more members of your family will be disappointed by the outcome. That happens in every family. But, with planning it may be possible to reduce the disappointments, and with effective communication it may be possible to decrease the upset feelings when things do not work out as your child had hoped they might.

You Love Him More

Children are very alert to differences in how they are treated. Such differences in treatment are inevitable, and sometimes they are even desirable, but they can form the basis for resentment and disappointment. We typically give different privileges, bedtimes, allowances, and responsibilities to children at different ages.

If you have two children, your treatment of each is based on age, maturity, and need. These decisions seem rational and wise to you, but may seem less fair to your child who sees himself as receiving the smaller portion of privileges, even if he is younger than his brother, who has been granted more age-appropriate freedom. However, your child can be helped to understand that some privileges are granted not because one child is loved more than the other, but because with age comes increasing freedom as well as increasing responsibility. Even though they may protest a bit, children can usually understand the justice in this formula as long as they find that they too receive their fair share as they grow up, and as long as they feel loved and valued by their parents.

Differences in privileges based on age may be relatively easy to explain to your child. It is harder to explain to children, especially when they are young, why one sibling receives the preponderance of parental attention because he has autism. Natalia Gonzalez's resentment that her parents were going to C.J.'s school meeting instead of hers is very understandable. She may have been correct in her judgment that she was not getting her share of parental attention, although that lack of equity was not due to a lack of love on her parents' part. To the contrary, Maria valued Natalia as a dear child and her only daughter. She also very much appreciated Natalia as her strongest helper at home. Nonetheless, Maria and Carlos Sr. had not worked out a balance of attention that would help Natalia feel she was getting her fair share of their time. Potential solutions to this kind of dilemma are considered in this chapter.

Together or Apart?

How do you feel about doing things as a family? Many parents believe that family activities should always be shared as a family unit. If they are going to the museum, the whole family should go, and if they are going to one child's Little League baseball game, everyone else should come along. When there is a child with autism, parents may feel especially strongly that this child should always be included in family events. They want to make it clear that the youngster is a full member of the family and the community, not someone to be left home with a babysitter while the rest of the family has a good time.

Although we respect the idea that everyone in the family should share family events, we believe it is important to think flexibly about who should be included in an event. If one child has a concert, and your child with autism is not able to sit quietly through the music, we believe it is usually more important for parents to go to the concert by themselves than it is to include the child with autism and risk disrupting an important moment for the other child. Every child needs a chance to shine, and sometimes a sibling with autism can cast a shadow that never allows another child to be the center of attention.

It is not only OK, it is probably very important to give each child some separate time with Mom, with Dad, and with both par-

ents together. That
is true in all fami-
lies, not just those
where a child has
autism. Perhaps
you have some fond
memories from
your own child-
hood of a special
event where you
were the center of
your parents' atten-
tion. You will want
to give your own children similar memories for the years ahead.

Time spent together need not be lengthy, or occur every day
with each parent, or revolve around a special event. But at least
several times a week, each child should know that he has the
opportunity to spend some private time with Mother or Father.
During that time, a parent should do her best to focus on that
child. For example, a father might take his daughter with him to
pick up a tool at the hardware store on Saturday morning. During the drive over and back, he would make her the focus of his
attention, using the kinds of communication skills discussed in
Chapter 4. During this same interval, his wife might be going to
the drycleaner, taking along their young son with autism.

One of the things the Gonzalez family decided to do to help
make sure they were touching base with the children each day
was to take turns putting the younger children to bed and to spend
time with Natalia before she went upstairs on her own at bedtime. One night, Carlos would work with C.J., talking with him
about the day just passed and planning tomorrow's routine, while
Maria tucked Gus into bed, taking ten or fifteen minutes to talk
with him, sing to him, and cuddle him. Later in the evening when
it was Natalia's bedtime, one of her parents would sit in the kitchen
with her while she had her night-time snack. This was a time for
sharing. By doing this consistently every night, they found they

had at least a few minutes a day of private time with each child. This focused attention helped them both be more alert to potential problems, and the children valued knowing they each would have some undivided parental attention each day.

Another approach Maria and Carlos might have taken would be to carve out a longer period of time with each of their children a few days a week, or to have a special shared activity such as playing tennis together each Saturday morning or going for a long walk on Sunday afternoon.

After they had their schedule for the children in place, Maria insisted that she and Carlos needed to make a plan for themselves. Maria knew that she needed to have some private time with Carlos if she were going to sustain the energy she needed for the children. So, they asked four people—Maria's mother, her aunt, Carlos's younger brother, and a good friend from high school—to each help them out one Saturday night a month. With these four helpers, each of whom understood C.J.'s special needs, Maria and Carlos were able to look forward to one evening a week that belonged to them. Just knowing that they were going to have this time alone made it easier to put up with the hassles of the week.

If they had not been able to turn to friends and family, the Gonzalezes would have been wise to consider professional respite care from a state or professional agency, or to ask for childcare support from church members or from special education students from a nearby college or university to meet their need for private time. See the section on "Using Resources," below for information about locating sources of support.

Being Together

It is important for a child to have special time with a parent, but it is also important to be together as a family. Part of what it means to be a family is to share things: to make group decisions about shared activities, to go places together, to have family jokes and family fun. It is important for your typically developing children to understand that your child with autism is part of that, just as they need to understand that sometimes they will do things separately from their sibling with autism.

Avoiding Embarrassment

Once your children reach preadolescence, they will probably become acutely concerned about how they appear to their peers. As a result, they may feel embarrassed to be seen in public with a sibling with autism. Your typically developing children may voice their embarrassment directly, or they may start to avoid family activities. These feelings should be listened to and respected as an expression of your child's experience. His feelings should not be the basis for dropping all family activities, but compromise may be necessary.

These feelings of discomfort are not unique to the sibling of a child with autism. Many adolescents want to "disown" their family and may lay down strict rules to their parents about how they are to be treated in public. For example, a teenager may ask his parents not to hug him in public, comb his hair, or use a family nickname. Similarly, parents may agree not to bring a difficult-to-manage child with autism to an important event for the teenager, but rather focus their family time on activities of a more private nature, such as riding bikes in the country or going on a camping trip. This way, you can protect the feelings of your teenager and still enjoy some shared times.

It may be a little confusing to your child with autism if his usually attentive brother ignores him when they on a family outing in public, but family life is a balancing act and you will need to decide when to ignore such things and when to intervene. Pick your battles!

Choosing the Right Activities

Finding activities that can be shared by your child with autism can sometimes be a challenge. Perhaps it is helpful to understand that the skills necessary for this kind of sharing can be mastered over time, just as other skills, such as speech or self-help

skills, are gradually learned and made more complex. Your child's teacher can be a valuable consultant in identifying activities within your child's abilities and in helping create programs to enable your child to learn the skills.

Examples of shared family activities that can be performed very competently by many people with autism are jogging, bowling, or bike riding. Shopping at the mall, preparing a special meal, or going to a movie may also be shared events. We know a family whose adolescent son with autism is fascinated by maps. He is the navigator on family trips, telling the driver when to turn and warning the passengers to be alert to upcoming scenic spots from the guidebook. This role keeps him happy and makes him an integral part of family trips.

It may take the person with autism longer to master the basic skills of an activity, but if you begin with modest goals and gradually build to broader objectives, it is reasonable to expect that many young persons with autism could go on a family bike trip or go jogging with a parent or sibling each morning. Indeed, we know a preteen with very significant autism who jogs with his Dad every morning.

If your child with autism has a hard time tolerating a family trip to the shopping mall, you may have to gradually build his tolerance for the experience. This can mean going only for a brief time in the beginning, and then slowly increasing the amount of time spent. It can also mean going at quiet times when there are fewer people and less noise and confusion. Initially, trips may need to include two adults with two cars, so one person can make a graceful exit with the child with autism, while the other completes the chores at the shopping mall. A ten-minute trip can grow each month to be a bit longer, until your child with autism is able to tolerate a full trip and to enjoy the experience.

Even when a child resists every new activity, it is important for parents to persist in introducing new things to do. People with autism need to learn to tolerate change if they are to function effectively in the world, and learning to manage the stress of change is therefore an important lesson of childhood. There are things you can do to help your child prepare for transition and novelty such as using activity schedules, as described in *Activity Schedules for Children with Autism* (McClannahan & Krantz, 1999) or social stories and other techniques, as described in *Reaching Out, Joining In* (Weiss & Harris, 2001).

Private Space

It is important to share time together, but it is also important that everyone in the family have time alone. Time alone may be the hardest commodity to come by in a family, and it may take a lot of planning to achieve the goal. However, parents need time away from their children, both as a couple and individually. You need time to renew yourself, time to enjoy your spouse, and time to feel a sense of yourself as a separate person. This is not simply self-indulgence. It seems to be important to good mental health to have the opportunity both to feel part of a unit and to experience ourselves as separate people. Although there are individual differences and cultural differences in how much private time we need, most persons who grow up in Western society have learned to treasure a certain amount of separateness.

Children, too, need some private time—time for their own hobbies, to watch the clouds float by, or to ride their bike to a favorite thinking place. That leisure is one of the things many of us treasure about our childhood memories. Having a sibling with autism may make private time a little harder to come by, unless parents are very sensitive to protecting their child from excessive demands. Childcare and household chores should not be so extensive that your child is denied free time.

It is important that children learn to carry their share of family responsibilities, including spending time with their brother or sister with autism, but responsibilities should not overpower the time a child needs to pursue his or her own life. Some children are so helpful to parents that it may be difficult to recognize that they have taken on too much responsibility and are paying the price by giving away some of their own childhood. The child who comes home from school to a load of chores and homework will have little opportunity to savor the freedom of childhood. This was in danger of happening to Natalia Gonzalez until her parents recognized the pattern and made some changes in their routine.

As part of your children's right to privacy, try to provide physical boundaries for the space, possessions, and activities of your typically developing children. Ideally this would mean giving each of your children a bedroom of their own, with a lock on the door, if necessary. If that degree of privacy is not possible and the room is shared with the child with autism, the siblings need some secure space. For example, you might put a lock on a closet, drawer, or footlocker where prized possessions can be stored without fear of damage by the child with autism. Likewise, if your child with autism always intrudes on his sibling's activities, you should either provide a separate play area or supervise the child in a different activity.

If your child with autism does damage a sibling's belongings, you should empathize with the sibling's anger, sadness, or frustration. You can do this by listening to your child's distress and conveying your understanding of his feelings. Your response should not stop here. When possible, the item should be replaced. To the extent that it is feasible, your child with autism should also receive some consequence for the destruction and be taught how to be more responsible. For example, he might have to spend time alone in his room (time out) and clean up the mess he made in his brother's room. Or, if he has a concept of money, take money from his own allowance to buy his brother a new item to replace the one he broke. The specific consequence will vary with the functioning level of your child with autism.

Everyone Contributes to a Family

We have focused a lot in this book on protecting children from becoming auxiliary parents with excessive responsibilities for their brother or sister with autism. The sibling should not have an adult disciplinary role for the child with autism or full-time childcare responsibilities after school or on weekends. Although siblings might issue mild reprimands (e.g., "stop tearing up the paper") or suggest alternative activities (e.g., "go play with your puzzles"), they would not be expected to put a child in time out or require him to clean up a mess. Nor should they be responsible for making decisions about the welfare of your child with autism.

Although children should be buffered from adult roles, they are part of the family and should carry their own weight. Even young children can do little chores such as putting their dishes in the dishwasher. Older children can make greater contributions such as clearing the entire table, loading the dishwasher, and putting the clean dishes away. They can also spend a brief period of time each day with their brother or sister with autism. If your child does not pose a management problem, an adolescent sibling could baby-sit in the evening or on a weekend.

Your child with autism should also start to contribute to the family at an early age. He might begin by putting his plastic cup on the counter after dinner, and gradually evolve to clearing the table, folding laundry, mowing the lawn, and so forth. Activity schedules can be used to help a nonverbal child learn chores such as emptying the trash cans in the house into a plastic bag, setting the table, or running the vacuum cleaner (McClannahan & Krantz, 1999). For example, he might learn to follow a series of photographs that depict step by step how to take items out of the dishwasher and place them in the appropriate drawers and shelves in the kitchen. Like your other children, he will need these skills in adult life, and he will be contributing to the entire family as he learns them. The other children in the family are less likely to resent him if he, too, has chores.

Using Resources

Perhaps as you have been reading this chapter you have wondered how it is possible for a person to do all the things we have described. Being able to spend time with each child, with your spouse, and by yourself can take a lot of juggling. Parents cannot always meet these needs by themselves, and single parents and parents with many children may find themselves overwhelmed unless they have help.

Informal Support

The parents of a child with autism should draw on every resource they can identify to give themselves extra help. You can start close to home, with relatives who might lend a hand. An aunt or uncle, grandparent, or cousin might be willing to stay with one or more of your children for a scheduled time each week or each month. Sometimes friends or neighbors will do the same. Many people find that members of their church or synagogue are happy to help out with childcare as well. These sitters will need a chance to get to know your child while you are present so they can feel at ease when you are away. Many parents begin by inviting a sitter over a couple of times to care for the child while they are home. This gives them a chance to check out the sitter and to train that person in working with their child.

Other parents of children with autism may be an especially useful resource. You could trade children for a day or a weekend, and know that someone who really understands your child is in charge. These families are also likely to have homes that are well "child proofed." Although this arrangement is hectic when you have the children, it is great when you are the one to get away!

Your emotional well-being is at stake, so do not be shy about asking other people to lend a hand. It makes people feel good and helps build a broad sense of community and belonging when we help each other. Both of us think the idea of self-sufficiency and rugged individualism that is so cherished by many people in western culture, when carried to an extreme, tends to undermine the sense of social connection so essential to a feeling of being part of a community. When we are allowed to give to one another, we build our community and contribute to a common good. So, calling on family and friends to lend a hand not only enhances the welfare of your family, it is good for the community as a whole!

Psychologists refer to family and friends as a person's informal support network. The more people you have available in your network to call on for help, the better your life is likely to be. It is important to build this informal network. It helps reduce your vulnerability to feelings of sadness and isolation when there are many hands to help out. It is better to have several helpers than only one or two, because there is a better chance there will always be someone available when you need assistance, and no one will get burned out from too much use. So, even if your mother says she wants to do it all, reach out to others as well. Similarly, an extended social network gives your other children many people they can turn to for help.

Sometimes there are difficulties in calling on family members to help out. For example, a research project done at our Center showed that grandparents tended to underestimate the seriousness of the impact of a child's autism on the family (Harris, Handleman, & Palmer, 1985). Perhaps because they do not usually live with the child, they may not understand just how hard it is to give him everything he needs. It may also be that you have not shared with the grandparents how difficult things can be for you. Just as your children wish to protect you from their feelings, you may be trying to protect your own parents. However, most parents with whom we have worked tell us that after they have shared their concerns with their own parents, these grandparents can become an important source of support.

It is helpful if you can be direct with your friends or relatives about what you and your family need. If your Aunt Lucy invites the whole clan for Thanksgiving, and the noise and confusion is too upsetting for your four-year-old with autism, you need to tell Aunt Lucy that. Maybe you can drop by for a short visit; maybe several people can take turns playing with your son in a quiet room, while others are part of the party; or maybe it will be easier to stay home on Thanksgiving, inviting just a few people to join you, and visit with your aunt on a quieter day. Other people may not know what you, your son, and the rest of the family need until you tell them. Creating an atmosphere where your child with autism is comfortable should help to ensure that the other children will have fun as well.

Formal Support

It is also important to call on your formal support network. These are the professionals in the community who provide services for persons with autism. For example, respite services can be a help to the whole family. In-home respite care involves having a trained person come into your home to provide care for your child with autism. Out-of-home respite can entail short-term placement of your child with autism in the home of a respite worker or a group home set up for short-term visits. For example, if you or your spouse needs to have surgery or if your family needs to go away, out-of-home respite would provide a few days of childcare.

Some people are shy about asking for respite care. We believe you should ask for everything you need. The more help you have in raising your child with autism, the better the job you can probably do for your child, your family, and for yourself. People who are chronically exhausted do not usually do as good a job of parenting as they could if they were rested. Your local Autism Society of America or ARC chapter should be able to help you find agencies that provide respite care. These respite services are often paid for in whole or in part by your state or county government, but you will need to register with a state agency and ask for the help. There usually is a waiting list for services unless a family is in an emergency situation.

Parent Support Groups

Parent support groups can help you learn to respond to the needs of your child with autism and to your family as a whole. They provide opportunities to share feelings, concerns, and coping responses. It can be comforting to realize the extent to which others share your experiences and understand what you are feeling. Other people's solutions may serve as guides to your own resolution of a problem. Sometimes other families may provide tangible support, such as joining together to take all of the children on an outing, or sharing childcare. Both of us are privileged to lead parent support groups at our Center and we see firsthand how valuable these exchanges among parents can become.

Parents talk about many things in support groups. Frequently the topics under discussion include the needs of siblings. Parents may share "guilty" feelings for not being more available to their other children, concern about how to explain autism to a young child, or fears about conceiving another child with autism. If you are looking for a good forum to explore your feelings and find emotional support from other people who will understand your experiences, a group like this can be a good bet. Some schools for children with autism offer parent support groups, and your local Autism Society of America chapter may also be able to help you find this kind of support.

For families who are geographically isolated or who prefer online conversation to a face-to-face group meeting, there are chat groups for parents and for siblings. The online addresses of these groups often change and your best bet is to do a search for "Autism Support Groups," as there are many that are available and they serve a variety of families with special interests. We found a number of links at the Family Village website (www.familyvillage.wisc.edu/lib_autm.htm).

Just one caution. As with every online resource, it is a case of buyer beware because you often do not know who operates the chat room or what special issues that person may be promoting. Neither of us has personally used a chat room as a resource and so we cannot endorse any particular one. That said, many families tell us that they do enjoy the easy access of an online conversation that they can enter and leave as their schedule demands and where they can often get useful advice.

One online alternative to the anonymity of a chat room is to make contact with one or two families at a regional or national autism meeting and establish an e-mail correspondence with them. This can be more enduring and personal than a chat room and may get around the problem of not knowing who is promoting a particular chat room. This can work for siblings as an e-mail buddy and for adults as well.

Sibling Support Groups

Support groups are not limited to parents. Siblings value the experience as well. Sibling groups can give children an opportunity to talk about feelings such as their anger at peers for rejecting a brother or sister with autism; fear of "inheriting" autism; jealousy; and resentment of the need to compete for parental attention. Sometimes it is easier to voice these feelings outside of the family, and other children can help to affirm the acceptable nature of uncomfortable emotions.

Unlike our parent support groups, where the participants set the agenda, our sibling groups have a planned sequence that extends across several weeks. These groups may consist of about half a dozen children of relatively close ages, such as seven to twelve years. The sessions are a combination of a group activity, group discussion, and snack time. The children may create a group drawing to illustrate the concept of individual differences in development, dictate to the adult leader a list of important questions about autism, or discuss some of their feelings about their brother or sister.

The first session always includes a brief meeting with parents and children together to discuss the plans for the group and lay the groundwork of confidentiality. At the final meeting we again include a session with parents. As part of this discussion, the group leaders review a list of items the children  identified as important for parents to know. This enables the children to share concerns as a group and allows parents to follow up on topics they wish to pursue at home. Although the specific format of the group will vary with the ages of the children, these kinds of activities can be quite helpful.

Don Meyer and Patricia Vadasy's (1994) book, *Sibshops,* provides specific information about what might happen in a sibling support group and how to get a group started. Additionally, we have found some of the activities in psychologist Debra Lobato's (1990) book *Brothers, Sisters and Special Needs* about sibling groups very helpful in facilitating discussion among children. Another valuable source of information and connection for siblings of children with varied disabilities is the web site for a national sibling support project: www.thearc.org/sibling support.

Your child's teacher or your local Autism Society of America chapter may be able to help you find a sibling group. Be certain it is run by someone with appropriate credentials such as a school psychologist, clinical psychologist, or social worker. At our Center, Beth Glasberg supervises doctoral students in clinical and school psychology who actually run the groups.

Closing Comments

Living in a family is one of the most difficult things we do. There are so many competing needs that must be met, and so little time to do so. Autism is not the only source of family stress, but if you have a child with autism, the demands of family life may be even more intense because that youngster needs so much extra help to meet his potential. The stress created by those demands can be a breeding ground for anxiety, tension, sadness, jealousy, and other painful emotions on the part of any family member.

Meeting the many demands of family life and helping each family member develop a fulfilling life may hinge in part on being able to draw on the resources around you. It makes good sense to ask family, friends, and professionals to contribute what they can to help your family thrive. If you are a single parent or a couple raising your children far from your own families, you may need to make an extra effort to reach out to your friends in the community. The more helpers you have, the better.

Fortunately, although family life is demanding, it can also be profoundly rewarding, and your children may emerge as richer adults for having been part of a family that included a youngster with autism.

Parents Speak

In keeping with this idea of occupying Matt's time, we have encouraged him to be independent and responsible around the house. He can cook, set the table, load the dishwasher, bring out the trash, etc. He has also developed interests in coloring, reading, arts and crafts, and helping his dad paint and work with tools on various home projects.

I sometimes think back to that powerfully energetic toddler. What I see today is an eight-year-old boy who is constructively busy most of the time, and happy being so. This has allowed me more time with my daughter, and a more relaxed and happy family life in general.

In giving direction to Matt's life, we have managed to take control of ours. When I now take some time for myself, I find it is not motivated by a desperate need, but by more of a healthy desire.

෴

I know I am not an expert at managing the complex balancing act within our family. I hope I am doing a decent job, but sometimes I'm not so sure. Unfortunately, parents of children with autism aren't given any special graces to deal with these circumstances. We are just ordinary people in very extraordinary situations.

I really feel there is a part of your life you must neglect to keep up with the other demands. In my case, I have never worked outside the home since Tommy's problems began. Some people may be able to work, but I always felt I could not give my all to both at the same time.

෴

It was hard for me at first, but I have finally started to ask other people for help. We applied to a local agency for respite care. We get twenty hours a month and that has made a big difference for all of us. My husband and I make it a point to go out together at least once a week, even if it is just for a movie.

One of the hardest things for me was letting my family know that I needed more help from them. My mom said I always seemed to have everything under control and she didn't want to intrude. Once I told her I could use the help, she was great.

෴

One of the toughest things for me about my son's autism has been how my family has reacted. When my parents heard that Dick had autism they just seemed to disappear. They never offer to sit with him. My sister-in-law asked me to leave Dick at home when they had a family party and invited all the other children. Those things just go right to my heart. So, I don't see much of my family, but it hurts a lot. When we talk in our parent support group about how some people have families who are so great in helping, I just want to cry all over again.

My husband and I have been trying to get together with other parents of children with autism and do things together. Sort of make a new family to help each other. It isn't the same as if my mom did it, but it helps to have friends who care.

When our teenager was thirteen, he went through a time when he did not want to be seen in public with us. If we went to the mall, he would walk about a dozen paces behind me so that people would not see him with me and think he wasn't "cool." I can understand that. I went through it myself when I was young. What was hard for me was that he especially did not want to be seen with his younger sister who has autism. She can be quite a handful, doing things like dropping to the floor and having a tantrum in the middle of a shopping trip. I wasn't sure if I should insist on her being with us, but I finally realized that if I pushed him very hard it might make more trouble.

He was good to his sister at home. If we were hiking in the woods or some place private, he would take care of her, but put him within fifty yards of another adolescent and it was a different story. That phase passed by the time he was fifteen, and now he seems very comfortable with us and with her. As I look back, I'm glad his mother and I did not push it too hard, and I'm glad we still managed to find some family things to do

that were private enough for my son to be at ease. Growing
from boy to young man is tough going.

My seven-year-old daughter who has autism broke one of her
brother's favorite toys the other day. He was very upset and
wanted me to punish her. At first I thought it wouldn't do any
good, but then I realized that even if she didn't learn anything,
my son would feel that I was standing up for him and it would
make him feel better. So, I sent her to her room.

My daughter's development and independence are as important
as my son's, therefore we try not to restrict her activities because
of his challenging behaviors. For instance, I take him to her
baseball games, running errands, church, etc., and work on
teaching him appropriate behavior, as painful as it is for all of us!
   Juggling their schedules is probably the biggest challenge,
especially since neither one understands why they have to go to
the other's events. Quite often my son tantrums and creates
undue attention toward us, which my daughter absolutely hates.

6 | Children at Play: Helping Children Play Together

The Laurel Family

Nine-year-old Rhona Laurel had a healthy zest for life. She delighted in her swimming prowess, was intensely proud to be allowed to ride her bike over the quiet streets of her neighborhood, and loved to play soccer with her friends on the empty lot at the end of her street. She was a well-liked girl with a number of friends. But at home Rhona was a different child. She played quietly in her room, often closing the door to exclude her younger brother, Nick.

Rhona had good reason to seek her privacy. Nick could be destructive, smashing a clay pot Rhona had made in crafts class by casually tossing it on the ground, or pushing her partially assembled puzzle on the floor into a shamble of pieces. When she would approach him to play, he would ignore her or push her away. He had been diagnosed with autism six months earlier, and although his behavior at home was getting better because of the good education he was now receiving, Rhona was still very cautious with him, afraid of his tantrums and of his seeming indifference to her.

One night when Mrs. Laurel was tucking Rhona into bed, she asked her daughter if she would like to learn how to play with Nick. Mrs. Laurel said that she understood how unhappy Rhona was about Nick destroying her toys and about not having him as a playmate. That day Mrs. Laurel had received a letter from Nick's school saying that they were starting a new project to teach siblings play skills, and wondered if Rhona would like to be a part of the program.

Rhona grew very excited and begged her mother to call the school that very minute. Mrs. Laurel laughingly reminded her daughter that it was night time and the school was closed, but promised she would call in the morning and tell them Rhona wanted to know more about their project for siblings.

Ted Kelly, Nick's preschool teacher, was delighted with Rhona's interest in play skills. He said Nick was learning a lot about simple play at school and it would be wonderful if Rhona wanted to help him play at home as well. He said he would come to the house and teach Rhona and Mr. and Mrs. Laurel how they could help Nick learn to play.

Rhona was excited about her time with Ted and her brother. She knew she was the star of this very important show, and she was determined to help her brother become a wonderful playmate. Ted suggested they start with a very simple activity, one Nick already knew how to do, so Rhona just had to teach him to play the game with her as he did with a child at school. Ted showed Rhona a few basic teaching skills and her parents watched so they could become her coaches. She learned how to make sure Nick was paying attention to her when she asked him to do something, to model for him how to do it, and to praise him when he got it right. With her mother and father cheering her on and helping her refine her skills, she quickly mastered the basic activities she needed to play with Nick.

Although Rhona still spends most of her time playing with her own friends, she now enjoys spending some time each day with Nick. They are playing simple games like catch, and rolling cars and making animal sounds. Sometimes Nick acts up a little and Rhona calls her father or mother to help her, but usually Nick enjoys his time with his sister and listens carefully to her directions. He gets excited when she calls him to play, and Rhona glows with the pleasure of being his companion at long last.

Introduction

Rhona's frustration at not being able to play with her brother is not unusual for siblings of children with autism. Neither is the

pleasure she felt once she mastered some basic skills and was able to engage Nick in simple play activities. Our own work with young siblings of children with autism has shown us time and again that many of them can master the skills they need to play with their brother or sister. Most importantly, this play can become mutually pleasurable for both children.

If you think that kind of play might be appropriate for your children, the information in this chapter may be helpful. We will briefly describe what is known about how siblings can help children with autism learn to play. We will also discuss some of the issues involved when children become "teachers." Then, we will share with you in some detail the procedures our colleague David Celiberti developed with Sandra Harris for helping siblings master the basic skills they need to be playmates. It is important to remember that the ages of both children and the degree of mental retardation (if any) shown by your child with autism will be important factors in determining how complex the play becomes.

Children as Teachers

A study by psychologists Nabil El-Ghoroury and Raymond Romanczyk (1999) looked at how parents and siblings play with a child with autism. They found that parents tried harder to engage their child with autism in playing than they to engage their typically developing children. The more impaired the child was, the more effort parents made to encourage the child to play. It appeared that parents were doing their best to compensate for the child's limitations. By contrast, siblings made fewer efforts to help their brother or sister compensate for lack of play skills and often made little effort to engage their brother or sister in play. It is encouraging to note, however, that the children with autism showed some interest in playing with their siblings.

This study suggests that if siblings had the necessary skills and interest, they might be able to engage their brother or sister with autism in some play activities and that the child with autism might show some reciprocal interest in the play. But how can your children acquire the skills needed to teach play skills to their sibling with autism? The short answer is that your children need to learn some basics of behavior management, as discussed below.

Behavioral Techniques as Teaching Tools

As you may know from working with your child with autism, the basic principles of behavior management are valuable educational tools. Several decades of research have helped to refine behavioral procedures into highly sophisticated methods for creating an effective learning environment. These procedures are now among the tried and true methods for helping children with autism learn (Harris & Weiss, 1998).

For those who are unfamiliar with behavior management, the teaching method involves:

- the use of rewards (positive reinforcement), such as hugs, tickles, or little bits of food;
- well-delivered instructions that are simple and brief, such as "Show me dog";
- physical and verbal guidance (prompts), such as gently guiding a child's hand toward the correct item and then removing that support as soon as possible or saying the first sound of a word ("ba...").

Research also tells us that consistency of teaching methods and expectations for behavior across settings and across people is very important to help children with autism learn. These children do their best when there is a high degree of consistency in other people's expectations for them. If a teacher is rewarding a child with praise and favorite toys for attempts to communicate, and her parents do not know that they should do the same, she will have a hard time learning to use her speech at home.

It was not long after professionals began to use behavioral techniques that they realized parents would have to become partners in their child's education to ensure consistency from school to home (Lovaas, Koegel, Simmons & Long, 1973). Failing to involve parents often means that children with autism will not transfer their skills from school to home and community. The importance of training parents in behavioral skills has become a fundamental assumption in the treatment of children with autism. It is clear that parents who provide a consistent home learning environment for their

child can make an important contribution to that child's development (Harris, 1983).

Given the valuable role of parents as teachers, it is not surprising that some people have wondered whether siblings could learn and apply behavioral teaching skills. The answer to that question is, yes, children can learn to use basic behavioral skills just as adults do (e.g., Colletti & Harris, 1977). However, that is not a very informative answer, because the question is really more complicated. To be fair to children, we need to ask what their "teaching" responsibilities for their sibling should be based on their age. Maturity becomes an important factor here. What we expect from an eight-year-old would differ sharply from what we expect from a fifteen-year-old, and our expectations for both children would differ from those for an adult.

Is it appropriate for siblings, especially when they are young, to become teachers for their brother or sister with autism? Should they be expected to spend an hour or two a day interacting with the child with autism? You may have concerns about imposing too many demands on your children. You might argue that children must be permitted to be children and not take on the obligations of parents or teachers. We share those concerns. We agree that children are not adults and should not have an adult's responsibilities. If we agree on that point, it then raises the next question. If children should not be burdened with the task of helping a brother or sister with autism learn to control disruptive behavior or master self-help skills, speech, or academic materials, is there still a meaningful role for them to play in relation to their brother or sister? We believe there is.

In fact, one of us (SLH) participated in a study to determine whether young siblings of children with autism could use simple behavioral skills to engage their brother or sister in play (Celiberti & Harris, 1993). We did not want to place the typically developing child in the role of auxiliary parent, but to help the children become more fully siblings. We discovered that not only are siblings with and without autism capable of learning to play together, such learning is often enjoyable to both children.

Teaching Play Skills

Psychologist David Celiberti has done extensive research developing methods to teach young children the skills they need to play with a brother or sister with autism (Celiberti, 1993, Celiberti & Harris, 1993). In his early work, Celiberti worked directly with the siblings, teaching them behavioral skills such as how to praise good play and how to initiate new games. Then he shifted his focus to teaching parents how to teach their children these same skills. This approach keeps the focus on the family.

His work shows that parents can be good teachers of behavioral skills. At least as important, he found that the children enjoy playing together. In his research Celiberti showed parents how to teach skills to their children and then measured the changes in how the children played. Celiberti found that the children became more skillful playmates and that they enjoyed being with their brother or sister with autism more after training than they had before.

In teaching children how to be playmates, Celiberti found it was important that the typically developing child wanted to learn the skills, rather than being pressured into doing so. He talked privately with each sibling before training to be certain it was something the child wanted to do. A few children decided they did not want to be part of the project. You will need to make that kind of assessment of your child's motivation. You should not pressure a reluctant brother or sister to learn these skills. Instead, explore why your child is hesitant and try to solve those problems. For example, your child may resent the time demands, be afraid of his sister, be concerned that he will not be able to learn the skills, or have angry or jealous feelings. You should only do this training if your child seems interested, and you should stop when he wants to stop.

Before you can teach your children how to play together, you yourself need to understand the basics of behavioral teaching. Quite simply—you can't teach what you don't know! The skills you should know include:

- how to give clear, simple instructions,
- how to reward good behavior, and
- how to give help when your child needs a prompt in order to respond.

There are good books you can read if you want to refresh your memory on training you received some years ago. For example, *Behavioral Intervention for Young Children with Autism: A Manual for Parents and Professionals* (Maurice, Green & Luce, 1996), *Steps to Independence* (Baker & Brightman, 1997), and *Right from the Start* (Harris & Weiss, 1998) are books parents tell us are helpful to them. You may hear different names for these behavioral techniques including *behavior modification* or *applied behavior analysis,* but these terms all refer to essentially the same methods of teaching.

If you have not had any training in behavioral skills, you may want to seek some parent training before you try to teach these skills to your children. The brief overview we are giving in this chapter will be helpful if you understand the behavioral basics, but it is not enough to make you skillful in behavioral methods if you do not already understand the essentials of these procedures. Incidentally, if you have never had any parent training, you will find it useful for many purposes and should do your best to obtain training from a competent person. A Board Certified Behavior Analyst, a psychologist skilled in applied behavior analysis, or an educator experienced in working with people with autism are the people who usually do this kind of training. Your child's school or the local Autism Society of America chapter may help you find such a person.

To teach your typically developing child to become an effective teacher/playmate for his brother or sister with autism, you should follow a series of three steps:

- First, remember to go slowly, do just a little each day, and be liberal in your praise of your children and your pride in yourself.
- Second, create the setting for teaching.
- Third, teach three basic skills:
    1. giving instructions,
    2. rewarding good behavior,
    3. prompting new skills.

Setting the Stage

Before you start to teach, you should set the stage for play between your children. Your children are most likely to learn and enjoy playing if you:

1. Select activities that are age appropriate and likely to encourage interactions between your children.

2. Don't overdo the teaching sessions.
3. Model appropriate play skills yourself.

Selecting Appropriate Activities

When choosing play activities, it is important to select toys that are colorful, attractive, and of potential interest to both children. Toys that encourage interaction, such as soft balls that can be thrown or rolled between two children, trucks or cars,  dollhouses, toy airports, garages, and doctor kits, are all toys that lend themselves to joint play. By contrast, crayons, scissors, and books and many electronic games lend themselves more readily to separate, parallel play that does not require much interaction. For the teaching sessions you are creating, choose toys that are likely to encourage interactions between your children.

In the beginning, it is a good idea to select activities that your child with autism already understands. If you are not certain that she knows how to play with a particular toy, find that out in a play session of your own. As we saw in the case of Rhona Laurel and Nick that opened this chapter, if the child with autism knows how to manipulate the toys, it is easier for the sibling-teacher to master the teaching skills. Later, she may decide to teach her brother new activities, but at first she should stick to things where she has a high chance of success.

Activities for Younger Children. Not only should the toys encourage interaction, they should also be age appropriate. Select toys and activities with an eye toward the developmental level of both children. The games should not exceed either child's skill level. For example, an older sister can create a "let's pretend" routine for her brother with autism. She might use a doll and some plastic food items to play house and assign her younger brother the role of feeding the doll. If that is too complicated for your child with autism, she can push cars or roll a ball with him. If your typically developing child is six or younger, pretend play may be more difficult for her to manage, and the children may engage in more concrete play together such as rolling balls, pushing cars, doing puzzles, and so forth.

Also keep the intellectual level of your child with autism in mind. If she has normal intelligence, she will be able to master more complex skills than if she has mental retardation. Children with mental retardation have trouble with the rules needed to play some games and with concepts such as sorting by color or number that may be essential to some activities. Your child's fine motor abilities should also be considered and materials selected that can be readily manipulated.

Activities for Older Children. Teenagers with autism are too old for the kinds of play we just described. The focus for a child this age could be on playing video games, ball games, age appropriate board games and card games, or learning the latest teenage dances. Adolescents can learn to use exercise equipment, jog, or go bowling.

Although we are presenting the material in this chapter in relation to younger children, the same behavioral techniques can be applied to these older, teenage-appropriate activities. However, if your typically developing child is much younger than the child with autism, the activities will have to be simple enough for the younger child. It is better that an activity be too easy than too hard. Your child's teacher probably has a wealth of information about appropriate games and activities and may even be able to tell you where to shop for materials.

Scheduling Play Sessions

Initially, you should schedule brief play times, perhaps ten or fifteen minutes once or twice each day. You should be present during these sessions because they are designed for teaching, and not yet for independent play. Later, as your children enjoy playing together, they will spontaneously seek one another out and may play for longer periods. However, as your child is first learning how to play with his brother or sister with autism, the experience may not be very rewarding and should be brief to maintain the interest of both children.

Modeling Play Skills

To teach your child the specific skills she will need, you should first model the behavior yourself. For example, if you are teaching her how to get her brother's attention, start the lesson by sitting down with your child with autism among the toys. Show your daughter how you make sure her brother is physically oriented toward you and looking at you when you give a direction. After demonstrating this for a few minutes, give your daughter a chance to practice the skill and praise her liberally for her attempts to do as you suggest.

As you coach from the sidelines, give lots of positive feed-back and gentle suggestions for improvement. For example, you might say, "That was great the way you got Don to look at you. Don't forget to be sure he is turned toward you when you talk to him." Often it is the adult teacher's praise that sustains the sibling during the process of learning these basic skills because the child with autism may still be quite unresponsive and not much fun as a playmate (Celiberti, 1993). So, be generous and specific in your praise. Tell your child what she did that pleases you and say it in a way that conveys your pleasure.

Each time you model good teaching skills for your child, you will include all of the components of good teaching, but your focus will be one skill at a time. If you are teaching your child to give good directions, be sure to emphasize this skill, even though you will also be rewarding your child with autism for responses to your directions. Shine the spotlight on one thing at a time. When your child masters the first skill, move on to the next. She may begin to learn some of the other skills just by watching you, but keep your own focus on one activity.

One important word of caution: young children should not be expected to deal with a sibling's tantrums, aggressive behavior, or other disruptive acts. Be prepared to intervene if these occur. It is important that your child feel safe in the play sessions. Some children with autism may go through a flurry of disruptive behavior while their brother or sister is first learning how to be a good teacher/playmate. Be sure you keep these behaviors under good control.

Giving Clear Instructions

Being a good teacher involves knowing how to give instructions. The first step to teach your child in giving an instruction is to make sure she has her brother or sister's attention. Her sibling should be looking at her or focused on the play materials when she gives the instruction. A child who is not paying attention is not likely to follow directions.

Instructions, especially for children with autism, should be clear and uncomplicated. Table 1 gives examples of good instructions that are clear and easy to follow.

Table 6-1 | Giving Effective Commands

1. "Put the man in the truck."
2. "Throw me the ball."
3. "Make the cow say moo."
4. "Push the car into the garage."
5. "Give me the doll."
6. "Give the doll her bottle."
7. "Make sounds like a kitty cat."
8. "Help me move the chair."
9. "Put your hands on top of the drum."
10. "Blow bubbles."

Instructions should also be given at a slow enough pace for the child with autism to respond. The sibling-teacher should learn that it is important to avoid repeating herself, giving the same command again and again. She should ask her brother to do something, and if he does not begin to comply within five seconds, she should give him a physical or verbal prompt to do so. (See "Giving Help," below.) She should not just repeat the command. This kind of "nagging" usually does not do much good. In fact, it often teaches a child to ignore directions rather than to follow them. For example, if your daughter asks her brother to "Make the sound of a cow" and he does not respond, she should say "moo" softly and praise him when he imitates her.

Avoid vague or complicated, multiple commands such as "Put it over there and then get another one and bring it to me." A better way to give those same instructions would be to use specific nouns and take it one step at a time. For example, say, "Put the car on the floor." Then wait for the sibling to do so; when he does, say "Get a car from the garage." When he does, say "Bring me the car." The simple and specific language in these instructions and the slow pacing make it more likely that a child can comply. For a child with more language and a better memory, commands can be combined. For example, your child could say, "Get the car from the garage and push it to me."

If your child has difficulty learning how to give effective instructions, spend some separate time with her playing the game of "Tell Me What to Do." In this game, which is a kind of "Simon

Says," first you give her an instruction and then she gives you one. You can give each other clear, but sometimes silly, directions to make this learning fun. For example, "Put the bowl on your head," or, "Put the glove on your foot." As you play, give her feedback on her instructions, praising her for being clear and specific. For example, say, "Great job, you told me exactly what to do," or, "You told me right where to put the car. You really know how to give good directions."

Being Rewarding

One of the essentials of being a good teacher is providing enthusiastic praise and affection for the student. Kids can do a terrific job at this! In teaching your child how to play with a brother or sister who has autism, your child must learn how to reward good play behaviors with specific praise. Saying things such as "Great throwing the ball to me," or "I like the way you put the doll in the carriage" are examples of verbal rewards that both praise and specify the desired behavior. Your child should learn to do this with energy and clarity.

If necessary, your child can pair her praise of her sibling with small treats such as pieces of cookie or pretzel. However, the play itself is intended as the most important reward and if food is not essential to learning, you need not use it. Instead, your daughter might pat her brother on the back or give him a tickle or a hug from time to time. Teach your child to give the praise and other rewards immediately after her sibling follows her instructions. If she does use food as a reward, you should also teach her to use praise each time she offers food.

After the children have played together for a while, you can provide a very natural food reward in the form of a snack such as milk and cookies or chips and juice at the end of their session. This is a reward for both children.

One useful teaching activity to do with your child is to help her make up a list of many reinforcing things she can say to her brother or sister (Celiberti, 1993). This should be done at a separate time from the play sessions. See Table 2 for some examples of rewarding statements. Help your child think of examples she can use with her own sibling. Do not forget to reward your daugh-

---

Table 6-2 | Being Rewarding

1. "Great job throwing me the ball."
2. "I like how you are feeding the doll."
3. "You're great at saying moo."
4. "Wow, what big bubbles!"
5. "When you bark you sound just like a puppy. Good work!"
6. "That is really a big tower. Great building!"
7. "Nice throw, Tom. You threw that really hard."
8. "Good talking. You sound just like the airplane pilot."
9. "I really like it when you play trucks with me."
10. "Thanks for bringing me the doll. You're a terrific sister!"

ter for doing this. You can praise her for her creativity in thinking of so many good sentences and let her know how much you appreciate her effort.

Another fun way to teach your child to be rewarding is for you to play a game with her and allow her to play the role of teacher as she does with her sibling. Let her reinforce you with a penny each time you make a correct response, and you in turn give her a penny for each effective rewarding statement she makes to you. Older children may not need these games, but will rely more on observing your model and getting feedback from you on their performance.

Giving Help

When children do not understand how to do something, we may give them physical or verbal assistance (technically called *prompts*) to follow the direction. For example, if a girl wanted to teach her brother with autism how to roll a toy car into a garage she might say, "Jack, put the car in the garage." She would give him two to three seconds to follow her instruction, and if Jack did not start to do so, she would take his hand, put it on the car, and push the car into the garage, saying, "Good, you put the car in the garage." Putting her hand over Jack's to guide the car is an example of a physical prompt.

It is important that children with autism not become too dependent on physical prompts, so we always make sure to give the child time to respond on his own (usually two or three seconds, depending on the child because some children are typically quicker than others), and then we provide no more prompt than is absolutely essential. Gradually, we fade the prompt until it is no longer required. For example, in this case the sister might make her touch softer, and then shift to just pointing at the garage, and finally fade the prompt entirely. She could also wait a bit longer—for example, four seconds and then five seconds—before offering a prompt. However, if her brother began to make a mistake, for example turning over the truck to spin the wheels, she would not wait to prompt him, but would immediately provide the guidance he needed to respond correctly.

Prompting can be a hard skill to learn. You should practice it with your child until she understands both when to prompt and how to decrease her prompt. This can be done with a combination of modeling by you and feedback to your child as she practices either in a rehearsal with you or a play session with her brother.

If your child with autism does not like to be touched, his sibling should not be expected to use these prompts. Rather, the first step would be to teach your child with autism to accept this kind of contact from you, and then to introduce the sibling's touch. Your child's teacher, the school psychologist, a physical therapist, or a certified behavior analyst may have suggestions about how to increase your child's tolerance of touch.

Finishing Touches

After your child has mastered how to deliver instructions, reward good behavior, and provide physical or verbal guidance, there is one more useful skill you can teach her. This involves rewarding spontaneous play behavior when it occurs.

So far this chapter has focused on teaching the child with autism to follow instructions. However, it is even more fun when he initiates the play himself. Your daughter should become alert

to these spontane-
ous events and re-
ward them with as
much energy as
possible. If she has
taught her brother
how to play catch
with the big round
ball and one day he
picks up a football
to throw to her, she
should praise him
with great energy.
Similarly, if they

have been playing with toy trucks and he picks up a toy airplane,
she should respond with enthusiasm to his initiation. The same
would hold true for new language. If her brother uses a new word,
she should express her delight.

This does not mean that your typically developing child is
always obligated to play with her sibling with autism, although
ideally she would respond with warmth even when she turns him
down. She can refuse when she wants to play alone, study, or be
with a friend. Parents should help the child with autism accept
these realistic limits. You might direct him toward an independent activity, and, if it is helpful, give him an activity schedule
with a picture showing him playing with his sister after he does
other activities such as watching a video and eating his dinner
(McClannahan & Krantz, 1999).

With Very Young Children

In working with families who have preschool children, we
suggest that, before teaching siblings to play alone with the child
with autism, family games be developed that involve all of the
children. This may help to make the children's interactions more

fun. An example is a game of "Come Here." This involves calling a child's name: "Zachery, come here." When Zachary comes, he is swept into the arms of an adult for a tickle, toss in the air, etc. The command may initially be given from only a few feet away, and the child with autism gently propelled toward the adult. Gradually, the distance is increased and parents may call from different rooms of the house, while partially hidden, and so forth. Typically developing preschoolers can enjoy the game, while the child with autism learns valuable skills in following instructions.

Similarly, a game of "Do This" in which nonverbal imitation is rewarded with hugs and applause can be a pleasure for both children. This imitation can be gradually expanded into that childhood favorite of "Simon Says."

With Teens and Pre-Teens

Older children may be interested in teaching their sibling with autism additional skills beyond the simple play skills outlined in this chapter. Again, however, we feel strongly that they should not be forced into the role of teacher if they would rather be doing other things with their time.

For older siblings, those who are preadolescents or adolescents, psychologist Bruce Baker (1989) offers an interesting approach to training siblings of children with mental retardation. Baker teaches these siblings basic information about their brother's or sister's disability, encourages group sharing of experiences, and offers the young people exposure to basic behavioral skills. However, he does not press the siblings to take on teaching responsibilities. Baker reports that children who completed his training program spent more time with their sibling than they had before training and that the quality of their interactions was improved. Thus, for older children, a modified "sibling as teacher" role may be useful. The skills that Baker teaches are the same basic behavioral teaching methods we mentioned above and that are described in more detail in *Right from the Start* (Harris & Weiss, 1998).

Your teenager may be happy to spend a half hour a day being a tutor for her little brother or sister. We know high school-aged youngsters who take an active and creative role in teaching their brother or sister with autism meaningful life skills. For example, one adolescent taught her thirteen-year-old sister how to pick out clothes that matched in color and pattern. Another young man decided to teach his brother with autism how to shoot a basketball and took on the activity as a personal, pleasurable project. In both of these cases, the initiation came from the teenagers, not their parents.

Closing Comments

Playing together is one of the important experiences that brothers and sisters share. It helps to build the sibling bond. When one sibling has autism, that play is often disrupted by the difficult-to-manage behaviors and lack of apparent response by the child with autism. Research suggests that siblings can learn how to help their brother or sister become a playmate. A sibling who can master the basics of giving effective commands, providing generous rewards for correct responses, and offering necessary physical or verbal guidance may find that these skills change difficult interactions into pleasurable ones. A parent who is skillful in the basics of behavioral teaching can help a sibling master these skills. Remember, though: it is very important that siblings are motivated to learn the skills and that playtime not become a burden for them.

Parents Speak

Over the years, some of the strategies I have used to develop the relationship between Matt, who has autism, and his sister Annie have revolved around play. Activities that involve music and song have been particularly effective—for example, "Row

Row Row Your Boat," "Ring around the Rosie," "If You're Happy and You Know it," and "Wheels on the Bus." I have also taught Matt and Annie how to dance together.

Matt has always loved playing chase games, especially being surprised. I took it a step further, and taught them how to play "Hide and Seek." Matt has also learned how to direct Annie in a chase game through different rooms in the house. He chooses the path she'll take to run and surprise him (i.e., "Annie come chase me. Go through the living room"). In addition, I used this idea of chase for pretend play as well, for example, "playing monster."

Finally, my children have benefited from some more sedentary activities, such as coloring, playing with Play Doh, and reading. When the children were younger, I naturally did the reading. Now that Annie is learning to read, she loves to read to Matt and he is encouraged to do the same.

༓

My daughter learned how to go about getting eye contact and the value of reinforcement. The important thing about the play program is that it was designed for her and other siblings. She now has the basic skills necessary to successfully have fun with her brother. These skills could be carried over to all settings. My daughter is now important to her brother's life—she can help him, play with him, laugh with him. What a boost to her self-esteem and family harmony.

༓

When you sent home a letter to my mom asking her about siblings, I asked her if I could write to you. She said sure, so here it is. I want you to know how great it is to play with Art. Sometimes I still get mad at him. But I like it when he learns to throw the ball with me and roll cars. Next, I'm going to teach him to pretend to be an animal like a dog or cat or lion.

෴

When I first started to get my kids to play together, I wondered if it was more work than it was worth. Eric, my boy with autism, can be a tough cookie, and he could really give my daughter, Sarah, a hard time. For a long time, I pretty much had to sit there and watch so I could pick Eric up and put him in time out if he got rowdy. But, gradually he started to enjoy being with Sarah, and now it is rare that he gets out of control. When he does, Sarah knows to call me and I put him in time out. It took three or four months to get it rolling, but now it works pretty well.

෴

Maurice and Ada play together in their own nonsensical way and have a unique bond. He knows she isn't a parent, but a full-time playmate, friend, and sometimes nuisance! She knows how much he can take and that if she crosses that line will receive a scream from him, or worse, an aggression. In turn, he also knows the boundaries with her.

෴

7 | An Adult Perspective: The Mature Sibling

The Garcia Brothers

Forty-eight-year-old Jose Garcia had worked with individuals with autism since his early twenties. He began his career as a special education teacher in classrooms for students with autism at a private school and, over time, had become involved in providing family support. At the time that I (BG) met him, he was a family counselor at the school where he had originally taught. His time might be spent on the phone answering questions from parents with a newly diagnosed child, or perhaps organizing a family activity day.

One day, Jose called to invite me to co-facilitate with him a discussion group for siblings of children with autism at his school. I eagerly accepted and we agreed to meet for dinner to plan the group activities. Although I had known Jose for several years and thought I knew a fair amount about him, toward the end of dinner he surprised me by revealing that he himself had a brother with autism. His brother was a couple of years older than Jose and had been institutionalized from the age of thirteen.

In describing his experiences growing up with his brother, Jose noted that his life as an adult sibling was very different than life would eventually be for today's young siblings. He explained: "I don't have a sibling with autism who is out here with me now living in the community. I hardly know him and I really don't see him. When my brother and I were kids, times were different, siblings were different. Having a sibling with autism was supposed to be a non-issue just because no one acknowledged it. Autism was not discussed with me. The biggest thing is, I think, that my feelings about my brother came out after I was an adult.

"If my parents struggled with issues about my brother when I was a kid, I never knew it. Nothing was ever shared with me. But don't judge them too harshly. Remember, that was back in an era when people didn't say words like 'cancer' out loud. There were a lot more secrets back then. But you know, even though we never talked about it, I guess I always knew on some level that my brother had big problems. I used to think that if I had a child like him, I could do better than my parents did. I thought that until I grew up and realized that autism was not an issue I'd like to have to face in my own life."

I found these final words ironic coming from a man who had devoted the last twenty years of his life to facing issues relevant to autism and doing his best to help individuals with autism and their families. In his own way, Jose faced autism every day.

Introduction

As Jose shared in his conversation, individuals who are currently the adult siblings of people with autism often had very different childhood experiences than the youngsters who will be the adult siblings of tomorrow. Recall that autism was not described as a distinct disorder until the publication of psychiatrist Leo Kanner's report in 1943. Furthermore, autism was not officially recognized as a diagnosis until the publication of the American Psychiatric Association's *Diagnostic and Statistical Manual - Third Edition* in 1980. Moreover, it is only recently that media attention about autism has increased to the point where even families who do not have a child with this disorder have heard of it.

The fact that there used to be no hope of improvement offered to families of individuals with autism would have had a significant impact on a sibling's experience. The message was that not much could be done to improve either the child's or family's quality of life if they kept their child at home. If the child with autism did not show an interest in playing with siblings, there were no established strategies to teach this skill. If the child with autism were aggressive toward siblings, there was little information about how to cope. In fact, there were few if any schools for children with autism, and certainly no services for their siblings. For many families like Jose's, institutionalization was the only option presented. Seeing your sibling sent to live on the ward of a state hospital and growing up living apart from that child leads to a very different type of relationship than living in the same house as your sister and seeing her making progress every day.

In spite of the urging of many professionals in the 1940s through the 1960s to place a child in residential care and "forget about him," some families declined this advice and kept their child at home. This presented a different set of challenges to the family. For example, in Shana's family, siblings and parents had to make a number of sacrifices to keep her home. Shana, age sixty, is an adult with autism who currently lives semi-independently. Although she has her own apartment in New York City, her sister assists her with her finances and helps her solve problems with household repairs, interpersonal issues, or other topics. Shana did not speak a word until she was four years old, but eventually  got a college degree and had a variety of job experiences ranging from pumping gas to working in an office. When she was very young, her mother took her from doctor to doctor and she was offered a range of diagnoses from deafness to mental retardation. Although professionals recommended institutionalization, Shana's mother refused. Instead, she worked tirelessly with her daughter to teach her to talk. Shana vividly recalls her mother holding attractive foods and drinks in front of her and refusing to provide them until she echoed her label of the items.

Shana required countless hours of her mother's attention and spent most of her time with her mother, as she had difficulty getting along with other people, whether children or adults. Shana has four brothers and sisters. Being one of five children usually demands a great deal of independence and ability to share attention. Although the other four children in the family had to defer to Shana, she rarely had to do so for them. Shana now knows that her siblings resented the attention she received from her mother, and as adults they have shared these feelings with her.

Even for adult siblings who grew up in the 1970s or 1980s and who may have had much more support than adult siblings of an earlier generation, autism has an impact on the sibling relationship in adulthood. Many of these siblings have grown up facing the challenges described in earlier chapters, day in and day out. Similarly, with an increased emphasis on inclusion in the community, today's adult siblings are more likely to have faced peers' questions and concerns than are their counterparts from earlier generations. These experiences may color siblings' feelings in adulthood when they reflect on their family memories. In turn, this may affect their decisions about what type of family relationships they want for their future. But it is also possible that today's young adult siblings may have been exposed to more positive events in their brother or sister's life than were siblings who grew up prior to the 1970s. They may have had more opportunities to celebrate accomplishments or to assist a brother or sister in learning skills that led to these accomplishments. These experiences may also affect adult decision making about family relationships.

When Siblings Take Responsibility for Their Own Relationships

When we are children, our parents orchestrate many of our interactions with our siblings. For example, they may structure the activities siblings share and ensure that each child also pursues independent activities. They may also determine how much time the family will spend together. When we reach adulthood, the sibling relationship is typically self-defined. It is the siblings who determine how often to call one another, how often to visit, and how much of their lives to share. These same decisions hold true for siblings of individuals with autism. While parents may hope for a certain quality of relationship between their children, the ultimate decision falls to the siblings.

When one has a brother or sister with autism, the relationship decisions may take on much higher stakes than usual. An adult sibling might have to decide whether to assume guardianship responsibilities for her brother with autism, or whether to introduce him to the man she is thinking of marrying. For example, we know adult siblings who have had to grapple with the problem of how their brother can attend their upcoming wedding when he may be quite disruptive at times.

People may choose a variety of paths in response to these challenges. Some siblings may assume a nurturing role and develop close, care-giving relationships with their brother or sister with autism. Others, like Jose, may lead more separate lives, showing their concern for their sibling in more indirect ways. In the rest of this chapter, we will discuss common themes experienced by adult siblings, as well as choices and challenges they may encounter. We will also describe resources available to help adult siblings with the unique challenges they may face.

Special Considerations for Adult Siblings: Establishing a Sibling Relationship

When a child leaves the family home and begins to live independently, he will typically have his first opportunity to truly define his relationship with his sibling. Parents may encourage adult children to phone or visit one another, but ultimately the siblings themselves negotiate their level of contact. In the case of adult siblings of individuals with autism, the responsibility of defining the sibling relationship may fall entirely on the typically developing adult. Many adults with autism may not be able to hop into the car and drive over to a sibling's for a visit or pick up the phone and call. It is the typically developing sibling who holds power over the frequency of interaction. Parents of these siblings often fervently hope that they will use this power to foster a close sibling relationship. Nevertheless, this may not always be the case.

As with any sets of siblings, some adult siblings of individuals with autism pursue a close relationship with their affected brother or sister and some do not. In our experience, we have come across siblings with a wide range of approaches to their relationships. Some young adults exercise their new-found independence by creating a life that is free from what they perceive to be the burdens associated with their brother or sister. Others describe strong feelings of love and attachment to siblings and wish to remain a part of their lives. Still others may feel responsible for their siblings and assume a care-giving role. We have found that there is no one outcome for adult relationships with individuals with autism. Furthermore, feelings and perspectives change over time. Because a relationship has one form today does not guarantee that it will not have a different form tomorrow.

Whichever choice an adult sibling makes is a legitimate one. Although it may be painful for parents, it is important that they accept their child's right to make these decisions. Siblings may feel very resentful if their parents try to dictate how much they should include the child with autism in their world. This can then act as a wedge between the siblings. Conversely, accepting a typically developing child's feelings and giving him full permission to experience those feelings is likely to promote a more healthy sibling relationship.

This does not mean that parents must condone all decisions made by their typically developing child about his sibling, but disagreements should be couched in terms that make it clear that parents respect their adult child's authority to define his own relationships. For example, a parent might say, "I understand how you feel about Johnny. It can be hard to include him

in your life—it requires you to make all of the sacrifices. I see that. But, I know that his successes have brought you a lot of joy as well, and that your visits really do make a big difference to him. For the sake of both of you, I hope that one day you'll decide that you'd like him back in your life." In the event that a sibling's choices and a parent's preferences do not match, and these conflicts cannot be resolved harmoniously, it can often be helpful to participate in family counseling.

Even after incorporating the suggestions above, a parent may find that his typically developing child wants nothing to do with his brother or sister with autism. This is not a parent's fault and does not signify a failure on the part of the parent. Many variables affect a sibling's decisions regarding his brother or sister with autism. Among other factors, children grow up contending with the influence of peers, the severity of their sibling's disability, and varying degrees of resources available to their family. Parents cannot claim sole responsibility for the quality of their children's adult relationships. With that said, it is worthwhile to note that in our experience, it is far more common for siblings to maintain loving, devoted relationships than it is for them to lose touch with one another. The vast majority of adult siblings that we meet are constantly seeking information about how to be more supportive of their brother or sister, rather than seeking separate lives. Parents should keep this in mind when they worry how their children will relate to one another in the future.

Siblings who desire to maintain a close relationship with their brother or sister with autism must identify what the quality of that relationship will be. As noted above, some siblings may choose to adopt the role of caregiver. For example, they may oversee living arrangements, financial matters, or health considerations. This can be an enormous responsibility, requiring a great deal of skills and information. If parents see that their typically developing child appears interested in assuming this role, they should be sure to pass on the benefits of their experiences as much as possible. It is best to start sharing relevant information while the typically developing child is living at home. This can be done without placing any expectation on the child about what his role will be in relation to his sibling as an adult. Parents can simply talk about what steps they've taken and how they were accomplished in the same way that they offer information about other aspects of their lives. A great deal can be shared in response to the question, "What did you do today?" Also, siblings can be invited to tag along on trips to hear speakers about advocacy and other related events.

Furthermore, both parents and adult siblings will need to negotiate well with one another if differences of opinion arise as to how best to serve the child with autism. Jointly discussing the pros and cons of all options can be helpful. During these conversations, everyone should make a conscious effort not to just try to convince the other person of their opinion, but to instead truly listen to what they have to say. If differences still cannot be resolved, consider seeking the advice of a neutral third party. Someone from a national or local autism agency may be able to share what they've learned from their experience.

Some siblings may wish to establish or maintain a friendship with their brother or sister with autism. These siblings may leave the caregiving responsibilities to parents while they share free time and activities with their brother or sister. Again, it is important for parents to be accepting of all types of preferences in this realm. Some parents feel very strongly that their typically developing child should be accountable for the well-being of their brother or sister with autism, and some parents work tirelessly to prevent their typically developing children from needing to assume this role. Despite the intensity of feelings on both sides, it is the sibling who will ultimately decide what part he will play.

Another defining aspect of a sibling relationship involves physical proximity to one another. Siblings who live on different continents will have more difficulty maintaining ties than those who live fifteen minutes apart. Because many adults with autism have difficulty traveling, siblings may feel an obligation to stay close to their brother or sister's home. This might affect decisions made about college, employment, or even about choosing a spouse. Balancing commitment to a brother or sister with autism with a desire for independence can be a difficult challenge for many adult siblings.

Special Considerations for Adult Siblings: Re-establishing Relationships

Sometimes adult siblings let their relationship with their brother or sister with autism lapse and then decide that they would like to have a stronger relationship. For example, we have met adult siblings who explain that they have been thinking about their brother or sister with autism but have let so much time go by that they are unsure of how to approach them. They feel as though their brother or sister would never recognize them. They wonder if it would mean anything to their brother or sister to see them again. They worry about their own reactions and what feelings might get stirred up.

There are no easy answers to these concerns. However, we feel that if someone is imagining what it would be like to see his brother or sister again, the outcome of seeing the sibling will likely be better than the outcome of not seeing him. Without taking a deep breath and going to see his brother or sister again, a sibling might develop regrets or always wonder what it would have been like.

Another reason siblings may find themselves struggling to reconnect with their brother or sister is because of a parent's death. While a sibling may have felt that his involvement was not needed in the past, after a parent dies, he may wish to step in and ensure a good quality of life for his brother or sister. Again, the sibling may wonder how to approach this task.

In this situation, spending time together is the best cure. Although it may not be easy to fill your time together at first, this will become easier. Find out what activities or foods your brother or sister has most enjoyed lately. If your sibling cannot tell you himself, ask a current care provider to fill you in. Pairing yourself with these preferred items will start your reconnection off on the right foot. Also be sure to find out any new skills that your brother or sister has accomplished, particularly related to communication. This may lead you to discover additional activities that you both can enjoy together.

Special Considerations for Adult Siblings: Financial and Legal Considerations

As noted above, some siblings will eventually elect to take over responsibility for meeting their brother or sister's needs from their parents. For this reason, it is especially important that parents acquaint siblings with the world of advocacy from an early age. This will prevent the need for the sibling to play catch-up in the event that this responsibility unexpectedly needs to be assumed immediately due to the loss of a parent. Ideally, parents and siblings should discuss what is involved in assuming caretaking responsibility long before it becomes necessary. Topics to discuss include:

1. *How have the financial needs of the individual with autism been met since he became an adult?* How will the financial plan change after the parents'

death? How much money, if any, will the siblings
need to contribute to meet his needs? Are there
changes that the parents or siblings could make to
their wills or life insurance policies to better
provide for the individual with autism, as well as
other family members?

2. *What needs does the individual with autism have for
a guardian at present and how might those needs
change over time?* If the parents have been acting as
guardian, is the sibling automatically the best
choice to take over as guardian? If the individual
with autism does have a guardian, what does that
individual do for him?

3. *What benefits has the individual with autism been
receiving from the federal government or other sources?*
Medical care? Housing assistance? Vocational rehabili-
tation? Social Security? What does the sibling need to
know about preserving those benefits?

In discussing these issues, parents and siblings would probably be wise to consult a lawyer who has experience in the disabilities area. Meeting the financial needs of a brother or sister
with autism involves complex and expert decision making. There
are, for example, limits to the amount of money an adult with
autism can earn or have in the bank, if he is to continue to receive
government benefits. And if trusts are not created correctly, laws
regarding funding for services can allow the state access to any
monies in the name of the individual with a disability.

There are also legal considerations in assuming responsibility for a brother or sister. For example, if a sibling wishes to
have the legal power to make medical decisions for his sibling
or to decide where his sibling will live, he must legally be ap-
pointed guardian for his brother or sister. This leads to more
questions, as there are different types of guardians with different types of authority for each. Again, getting competent legal
counsel for these issues is essential.

Finally, adults with disabilities have special rights with regard to employment, housing, health care, and other areas. In order to be an effective advocate for a brother or sister, a sibling needs to become well versed with laws pertaining to individuals with disabilities. National agencies, such as the Autism Society of America and state agencies, such as your state Protection & Advocacy agency (see Resources) can be helpful in obtaining updated, easy-to-read summaries of advocacy information. There may also be state autism agencies or organizations that can help point you in the right direction.

Special Considerations for Adult Siblings: Marriage and Family

Growing up with a brother or sister with autism can influence a person's decisions about establishing intimate relationships and possibly getting married. For example, as a child, a sister may have often encountered people who were not accepting of her brother with autism and this may have led her to be cautious in making connections with people. This history may lead her to require very high standards of trust before bringing a prospective mate to meet her family. Child siblings often report feelings of anxiety about bringing friends over, or embarrassment about being teased by a peer. Adult siblings may experience these feelings as well with the added intensity of the strong feelings they have for their prospective partner.

There may be added complications if a young adult sibling decides he will eventually assume primary responsibility for his sibling with autism. Knowing that his parents will likely die before his brother with autism, a sibling may anticipate assuming a caregiving role for his brother when that becomes necessary. This may involve a great deal of time and money to ensure his brother's well being. For some adult siblings, it may even mean that their brother or sister will live with them. The consequences of this choice would have to be shared with a life partner, and thus may limit one's selection of potential partners.

There are positive, as well as more challenging aspects, to forming intimate relationships as an adult sibling of an individual with autism. For example, siblings of people with disabilities often describe more childhood experiences than usual requiring them to be nurturing, accepting, and patient. These are skills that enhance any intimate relationship. Similarly, in our experience, many parents and siblings report a  greater appreciation of life's small accomplishments and simple experiences as a benefit of living with an individual with autism. Families of individuals with autism often take less for granted than do other people. If adult siblings apply this perspective to their interactions with significant others, their relationships can be expected to benefit.

Being an adult sibling of an individual with autism may also influence childbearing choices. Adult siblings face tough questions regarding their possible genetic makeup. Although the specific causes of autism are not known, what is known is that for many people with autism there is a genetic component (Folstein & Rosen-Sheidley, 2001). Unless he is an identical twin, there is a low probability that a sibling of an individual with autism will himself have a child with autism. Nevertheless, sharing the genetic heritage of an individual with autism does increase the risk of having a child with this disability compared to other adults. Because of this risk, many adult siblings experience more anxiety than their peers when making decisions about having children.

Furthermore, other family members may share their fears. For example, in the course of inviting families to participate in the research on siblings' understanding of autism described in Chapter 2, one mother asked whether her seventeen-year-old daughter would be asked how people develop autism. After hearing that the question would be included, she explained that she could not have her daughter participate for fear that she would begin to think about genetics, which in turn might lead her to decide against having her own children.

In contrast, some aspects of growing up with a brother or sister with autism may make the transition to the role of parenting easier. During a recent meeting of a sibling group for adolescents, six teenage girls ranging in age from fifteen to seventeen all agreed that the best thing about growing up with a sibling with autism was the preparation that they were receiving for parenthood. They explained that either through programs at their siblings' school, or through information that their parents had shared, they had learned how to be good teachers for children. They talked about their ability to teach shoe tying and tooth brushing, and knowing how to keep a sibling "well-behaved." The teens explained that these skills, coupled with the patience that they had learned through experience with their brother or sister, would surely help them be better parents. In fact, they joked about how friends with typically developing siblings often seemed so incompetent when babysitting.

Adult siblings who do decide to have children of their own will be faced with the challenge of explaining autism to their own children. Unless they choose to keep their sibling with autism out of their life, they will probably have to explain things such as why Uncle Tim seems so shy or why Aunt Elizabeth doesn't seem to talk like other adults. Having themselves been faced with the task of understanding autism as a child, they may be more sensitive to the needs and concerns of their own children, and may fall back on the models provided by their own parents' explanations in how to best meet their child's needs. We know several families in which an uncle or aunt with autism is included in family outings and holiday celebrations. The nieces and nephews have grown up with these experiences and seem to treat them very matter-of-factly.

When Adults with Autism Have Children

Sometimes an adult with autism will marry and have children of his own, only to find the process of child rearing to be quite overwhelming. In rare instances, a sibling of the person with autism may then find himself having to assume a childcare role for a niece or nephew born to his brother or sister. This was the case with Giselle's family:

> Giselle is a thirty-five-year-old woman with Asperger's disorder. She was married for a short time, and became pregnant. Her husband divorced her soon afterwards and then dropped out of both her life and her daughter's. Due to difficult social interaction with peers as well as challenges related to anger management, Giselle has been unable to sustain independent employment. She is financially dependent on Social Security checks and lives in a group home. These factors prevent her from caring for her daughter in a way that she feels would be effective. Additionally, her daughter, now six, requires some specialized supports, as she too has been diagnosed with Asperger's disorder.
>
> Because of these challenges, Giselle's brother and sister-in-law agreed to raise her daughter. This way, Giselle can visit her daughter frequently and maintain a relationship with her, while her brother takes over the financial and caretaking responsibilities. While Giselle's brother and his wife undoubtedly derive pleasure from their close relationship with their niece, the decision to assume responsibility for a sibling's child must have been a difficult one.

In addition to highlighting the special roles that may be assumed by siblings of individuals with autism and related disorders, Giselle's story also highlights the importance of support around reproductive concerns. Although sex education and family planning are important and challenging issues in all families, they take on added complexity for individuals with autism. Identifying the best choices can involve varied and intricate considerations. Parents and adult siblings can be very helpful guides through this process for their family member with autism.

Special Considerations for Adult Siblings: Choosing a Career

Like other adults, siblings of individuals with autism must make decisions regarding careers. This too can be affected by the experience of growing up with a brother or sister with autism. As we saw with Jose, many adult siblings of individuals with developmental disabilities choose a career in a helping profession (Seligman & Darling, 1997). There are many successful special educators, psychologists, speech therapists, physical therapists, physicians, and others in helping occupations who

are adult siblings of people with disabilities. In fact, several of our colleagues entered the field of autism because of firsthand experiences in their own families. We also know several siblings of children with autism who decided to become special education teachers or psychologists because of what they learned as children. Given the benefits of having a sibling with autism listed by the teenagers in the adolescent sibling group described above, these career choices are not surprising. However, many other brothers and sisters will choose to go into a variety of careers based on their own interests, and these choices, too, are often good ones. Any vocational choice can be healthy if it is freely made.

Some siblings may face expectations, either from themselves or from parents, that conflict with pursuing a dream career. They may feel guilty about moving away from their family of origin because they will not be able to spend time with their brother or sister with autism or will not be available to help their parents with related responsibilities. For example, if a sibling from North Dakota wants to pursue a career as an investment banker and the best opportunities are in New York, it might be difficult if not impossible for her brother to visit her there. Furthermore, this sibling may typically help manage her brother's challenging behaviors or do the household cleaning to free up her parents to work on educational programs with her brother or sister. When that opportunity to head to New York comes through, it may lead to conflicting emotions.

In this type of situation, it is important to keep in mind that there are many ways to give support to the family. Long distance siblings can be just as helpful as local siblings but in different ways. A phone call offering to lend an ear to a parent who may be facing difficult advocacy challenges can be invaluable. Sending recent information about autism to parents via e-mail may also be helpful. Mailing photos or a favorite video to a brother or sister can help maintain a connection. Even spending a few years focused entirely on one's own professional endeavors can be beneficial to a family, considering that the greatest gift a sibling can offer a loved one is to create a fulfilled, independent life for himself.

Resources for Adult Siblings

While child siblings of today may meet other siblings of children with autism through their brother's school or a local sibling discussion group, these options are rarely available for adult siblings. Especially if a sibling is geographically separated from his brother and his service providers, he may be disconnected from the autism community. This can lead to feelings of isolation for the adult sibling.

One source of information and connection that may meet the needs of adult siblings is the Sibling Support Project. This group offers online information and support to siblings of individuals with autism. General information about sibling issues can be found at their web site: www.thearc.org/siblingsupport. Additionally, there are chat rooms and information geared specifically toward adult siblings on the "Sibnet" portion of their site. This web site also offers information about events for adult siblings that may be taking place around the nation.

Local agencies that serve individuals with autism and related disabilities may also have information relevant to adult siblings. For example, the South Carolina Department of Disabilities and Special Needs has a highly informative web site devoted specifically to the needs of adult siblings: www.state.sc.us/ddsn/pubs/matters/matters.htm. Consider this site and those of other local agencies to review and obtain additional information about a variety of issues that might be important to adult siblings.

Counseling services from a psychologist or other therapist familiar with autism can provide another helpful resource for siblings. Through counseling, a sibling might explore the impact of his brother's or sister's disability on his life path and the decisions that he has made, or the influence of experiences with his sibling on choices that he needs to make in the future. Some siblings may first fully realize in adulthood that their experiences as a brother or sister were not the same as those of their peers. This realization may trigger feelings of loss, disappointment, or even anger. Thinking through these emotions with a competent therapist can be extremely helpful. Other siblings may need support around feelings related to the relationship that they have created with their brother or sister. For example, assuming care-taking responsibilities may be overwhelming at first and involves a shift in one's sense of identity.

It is important for siblings to remember that participation in counseling does not imply that one has a "problem," but it does go a long way in helping people feel good about themselves and preventing the onset of any serious problems. For referrals to local counselors with relevant expertise, contact local autism agencies.

Closing Comments

Regardless of the quality of the relationship, our brothers and sisters are part of our emotional lives forever. For the adult who has a sibling with autism, this relationship poses both special challenges and special rewards. When siblings grow up with an understanding of autism and with parents who enable them to cope well with having a relationship with a sibling with a disability, the challenges of adulthood, while still demanding, may be much less daunting than for siblings who grow up in less communicative and supportive families. Today's siblings are fortunate to live at a time when society is much more open than in the past about "secrets" such as disability or illness. This openness encourages parents to share information and feelings with children in ways that respect the child's developmental understanding and emotional readiness to cope with new knowledge.

Parents and Siblings Speak

I worry about when they are both teenagers and my daughter will want more privacy. I don't think my son will understand concepts like nudity, good manners, personal space, etc. She may become distant from him. I hope I'll be understanding of this and realize that in the future they will become close again.

⟡

My husband and I do not want the burden of taking care of our son to fall on our daughter. We hope she will be able to live her life as if her brother were "neuro-typical."

⟡

As she gets older, we worry about her future and have concerns (should she want to start a family) about the genetic
aspect of the disorder.

‍∿

When I was a kid, it seemed to me that my brother Rich, who
has autism, got the lion's share of attention in our house. Now
that I am an adult, I can understand the jam my parents were
in, but it was tough for me when I was younger. I love Rich,
and my wife and I invite him to spend holidays with us, but I
try to make sure my own kids understand why Uncle Rich
needs so much of Dad's time when he visits.

I guess it isn't an accident that I ended up as a pediatrician. All the time I was growing up, I kept praying there would
be a way to cure Rich.

‍∿

I will always be grateful to my parents for how they talked to
me when I was kid. They told me about my brother's autism,
and they seemed to be able to understand when I teased him or
pushed him around a little. I mean they didn't say it was OK,
but they didn't do a real guilt trip either. They would punish
me the same way my best friend got punished when he would
tease his little sister. No more and no less. Plus, they would
help me find things I could do that would give me a way to
play with my brother. It wasn't ideal, and I think they made
mistakes like all parents do, but I always knew they would
listen to me and try to be fair. I appreciate that all the more
now that I'm grown and know how hard it must have been on
them raising the two of us and him having autism.

‍∿

RESOURCE GUIDE

The Arc
1010 Wayne Ave., Ste. 650
Silver Spring, MD 20910
301-565-3842
www.thearc.org
A grassroots organization that works to include all children and adults with cognitive and developmental disabilities in every community. Sponsors local chapters that provide support and offers a wide variety of publications on its web site.

Asperger Syndrome Coalition of the United States
P.O. Box 351268
Jacksonville, FL 32235-1268
866-4-ASPRGR
www.asperger.org
A national nonprofit organization committed to providing up-to-date and comprehensive information on Asperger syndrome and related conditions. Offers articles as well as contact information for support groups that serve people with AS and related conditions and their families.

Autism Society of America
7910 Woodmont Ave., Ste. 300
Bethesda, MD 20814
301-657-0881; 800-328-8476
www.autism-society.org
A national organization of parents and professionals that promotes a better understanding of autism, encourages the development of services, supports autism-related research, and advocates on behalf of people with autism and their families. Has a national network of local chapters and acts as an information clearinghouse.

Autism Society Canada
P.O. Box 635
Fredericton, New Brunswick
Canada E3B 5B4
506-363-8815
www.autismsocietycanada.ca
    A national nonprofit organization committed to advocacy, public education, information and referral, and advocacy. Has links to provincial autism societies and information related to Canadians with autism.

Behavior Analyst Certification Board
519 E. Park Ave.
Tallahassee, FL 32301
www.bacb.com
    Website provides details about credentials necessary to be certified as a behavior analyst and can assist in locating a behavioral consultant.

Family Village: A Global Community of Disability-Related Resources
www.familyvillage.wisc.edu
    This website has a great deal of information about disability and the family, autism, and other disabilities, as well as links to other sites, online support groups, listservs, etc.

National Autism Society (England)
393 City Rd.
London EC1V 1NG
United Kingdom
+44 (0)20 7833 2299
www.nas.org.uk
    The UK's foremost organization for people with autism and those who care about them. Organization can provide information on support groups for parents and siblings and "holiday facilities" specifically for young people with autism, and website offers information geared specifically to siblings as well as to parents.

Protection and Advocacy Program for People with Developmental Disabilities (PADD)
Administration on Developmental Disabilities
U.S. Dept. of Health and Human Services
200 Independence Ave., SW
Washington, DC 20201
202-690-6590

www.acf.hhs.gov/programs/add/states/p&a.htm

Under PADD, each state has its own Protection & Advocacy office, which is mandated to empower, protect, and advocate on behalf of people with developmental disabilities. The P&As provide information and referral services and can provide legal assistance in advocating for the rights of people with disabilities. Website has links to each state's P&A office.

Sibling Support Project
The Arc
www.thearc.org/siblingsupport

Sponsors listserv for young siblings (SibKids) and for adult sibs (Sibnet). Has database of sibling programs; conducts workshops for siblings

REFERENCES

Alessandri, M. (1992). *The influence of sex-role orientation on the marital adjustment and degree of parental involvement in family work: A comparison of mothers and fathers of children with autism and mothers and fathers of normally developing children.* Unpublished doctoral dissertation, Rutgers, The State University of New Jersey, Piscataway, NJ.

American Psychiatric Association (2000). *Diagnostic and statistical manual of mental disorders.* 4th Ed. Text Revision. Washington, DC: Author.

Baker, B.L. (1989). *Parent training and developmental disabilities.* Washington, DC: American Association on Mental Retardation.

Baker, B.L. & Brightman, A.J. (1997). *Steps to independence: Teaching everyday skills to children with special needs.* Baltimore, MD: Paul H. Brookes.

Bank, S.P. & Kahn, M.D. (1982). *The sibling bond.* New York: Basic Books.

Berry, S.L., Hayford, J.R., Ross, C.K., Pachman, L.M., & Lavigne, J.V. (1993). Conceptions of illness by children with Juvenile Rheumatoid Arthritis: A cognitive developmental approach. *Journal of Pediatric Psychology, 18,* 83-97.

Bibace, R. & Walsh, M.E. (1979). Developmental stages in children's conceptions of illness. In G.C. Stone & N.E. Adler (Eds.) *Health Psychology* (pp.285-301). San Francisco: Jossey Bass.

Bibace, R. & Walsh, M.E. (1980). Development of children's concepts of illness. *Pediatrics, 66,* 912-917.

Boer, F., Goehardt, A.W., & Terffers, P.D.A. (1992). Siblings and their parents. In F. Boer & J. Dunn (Eds.), *Children's sibling relationships: Developmental and clinical issues* (pp. 41-54). Hillsdale, NJ: Erlbaum Associates.

Bondy, A. & Frost, L. (2001). *A picture's worth: PECS and other visual communication strategies in autism.* Bethesda, MD: Woodbine House.

Brodzinsky, D. & Schechter, M.(Eds.) (1990). *The psychology of adoption.* New York: Oxford University Press.

Burbach, D.J., & Peterson, L. (1986). Children's concepts of physical illness: A review and critique of the cognitive developmental literature. *Health Psychology, 5,* 307-325.

Buhrmester, D. (1992). The developmental course of sibling and peer relationships. In F. Boer & J. Dunn (Eds.), *Children's sibling relationships: Developmental and clinical issues* (pp. 1-40). Hillsdale, NJ: Erlbaum Associates.

Carandang, M.L.A., Folkins, C.H., Hines, P.A., & Steward, M.S. (1979). The role of cognitive level and sibling illness in children's conceptualizations of illness. *American Journal of Orthopsychiatry, 49,* 474-481.

Celiberti, D.A. (1993). *Training parents of children with autism to promote sibling play: Randomized trials of three alternative training interventions.* Unpublished doctoral dissertation, Rutgers, The State University of New Jersey, Piscataway, NJ.

Celiberti, D.A. & Harris, S.L. (1993). The effects of a play skills intervention for siblings of children with autism. *Behavior Therapy, 24,* 573-599.

Cicirelli, V.G. (1995). *Sibling relationships across the life span.* New York: Plenum Press.

Colletti, G. & Harris, S.L. (1977). Behavior modification in the home: Siblings as behavior modifiers, parents as observers. *Journal of Abnormal Child Psychology, 1,* 21-30.

Dunn, J. (1992). Sisters and brothers: Current issues in developmental research. In F. Boer & J. Dunn (Eds.), *Children's sibling relationships: Developmental and clinical issues* (pp. 1-40). Hillsdale, NJ: Erlbaum Associates.

El-Ghoroury, N.H. & Romanczyk, R.G. (1999). Play interactions of family members towards children with autism. *Journal of Autism and Developmental Disorders, 29,* 249-258.

Erikson, E.H. (1963). *Childhood and society.* 2nd Ed. New York: Norton.

Folstein, S.E. & Rosen-Sheidley, B. (2001). Genetics of autism: Complex aetiology for a heterogeneous disorder. *Nature Reviews, 2,* 943-955.

Forgatch, M. & Patterson, G. (1989). *Parents and adolescents living together: Part 2: Family problem solving.* Eugene, OR: Castalia Publishing Co.

Glasberg, B.A. (1998). *The development of a child's appraisal of a sibling's autism.* Unpublished doctoral dissertation, Rutgers University, Piscataway, New Jersey.

Glasberg, B.A. (2000). The development of siblings' understanding of autism and related disorders. *Journal of Autism and Developmental Disorders, 30* (2), 143–156.

Grissom, O.M. & Borkowski, J.G. (2002). Self-efficacy in adolescents who have siblings with or without disabilities. *American Journal on Mental Retardation, 107,* 79-90.

Harris, S.L. (1983). *Families of the developmentally disabled: A guide to behavioral intervention.* Elmsford, NY: Pergamon Press.

Harris, S.L., Handleman, J.S., & Palmer, C. (1985). Parents and grandparents view the autistic child. *Journal of Autism and Developmental Disorders, 15,* 127-137.

Harris, S.L., & Weiss, M. J. (1998). *Right from the start: Behavioral intervention for young children with autism.* Bethesda, MD: Woodbine House.

Holmes, N. & Carr, J. (1991). The pattern of care in families of adults with a mental handicap: A comparison between families of autistic adults and Down syndrome adults. *Journal of Autism and Developmental Disorders, 21,* 159-176.

Jenkins, J. (1992). Sibling relationships in disharmonious homes: Potential difficulties and protective effects. In F. Boer & J. Dunn (Eds.), *Children's sibling relationships: Developmental and clinical issues* (pp. 125-138). Hillsdale, NJ: Erlbaum Associates.

Kaminsky, L. & Dewey, D. (2001). Sibling relationships of children with autism. *Journal of Autism and Developmental Disorders, 31,* 399-410.

Kanner, L. (1943). Autistic disturbances of affective contact. *Nervous Child, 2,* 217-240.

Lobato, D. (1990). *Brothers, sisters and special needs.* Baltimore, MD: Paul H. Brookes.

Lovaas, O.I., Koegel, R., Simmons, J.Q., & Long, J.S. (1973). Some generalization and follow-up measures on autistic children in behavior therapy. *Journal of Applied Behavior Analysis, 6(1),* 131-166.

Maurice, C. (1993). *Let me hear your voice.* New York: Alfred A. Knopf.

Maurice, C., Green, G. & Luce, S.C. (Eds.) (1996). *Behavioral intervention for young children with autism: A manual for parents and professionals.* Austin, TX: Pro-Ed.

McClannahan, L.E. & Krantz, P.J. (1999). *Activity schedules for children with autism: Teaching independent behavior.* Bethesda, MD: Woodbine House.

McHale, S.M. & Harris, V.S. (1992). Children's experiences with disabled and nondisabled siblings: Links with personal adjustment and relationship evaluations. In F. Boer & J. Dunn (Eds.), *Children's sibling relationships: Developmental and clinical issues* (pp. 83-100). Hillsdale, NJ: Erlbaum Associates.

McHale, S.M., Sloan, J., & Simeonsson, R.J. (1986). Sibling relationships of children with autistic, mentally retarded, and nonhandicapped brothers and sisters. *Journal of Autism and Developmental Disorders, 16,* 399-413.

Meyer, D.J., & Vadasy, P.F. (1994). *Sibshops: Workshops for siblings of children with special needs.* Baltimore, MD: Paul H. Brookes.

Osborne, M.L., Kistner, J.A., & Helgemo, B. (1993). Developmental progression in children's knowledge of AIDS: Implications for educational and attitudinal change. *Journal of Pediatric Psychology, 18,* 177-192.

Piaget, J. (1929). *The child's conception of the world.* New York: Harcourt Brace Jovanovich.

Powers, M.D. (Ed.) (2000). *Children with autism.* 2nd Ed. Bethesda, MD: Woodbine House.

Rodrique, J.R., Geffken, G.R., & Morgan, S.B. (1993). Perceived competence and behavioral adjustment of siblings of children with autism. *Journal of Autism and Developmental Disorders, 23,* 665-674.

Schonfeld, D.J., Johnson, S.R., Perrin, E.C., O'Hare, L.L., & Cicchetti, D.V. (1993). Understanding of Acquired Immunodeficiency Syndrome by elementary school children – A developmental survey. *Pediatrics, 92,* 389-395.

Seligman, M. & Darling, R.B. (1997). *Ordinary families, special children.* 2nd Ed. New York: Guilford Press.

Weiss, M.J. & Harris, S.L. (2001). *Reaching out, joining in: Teaching social skills to young children with autism.* Bethesda, MD: Woodbine House.

INDEX

Access, 8
Activities, play, 135-36
Activity schedules, 112, 115, 144
Activity Schedules for Children with Autism, 112
Adolescent siblings
  as teachers, 145-46
  changes in, over time, 3, 11
  concerns of, 22, 69-70
  independence in, 18-19, 70-71
  role in behavior management, 68-69
  understanding of autism, 42, 67-68
Adoption, 5
Adult siblings
  career choices, 164-65
  caretaking responsibilities of, 21, 72, 154, 156
  financial and legal considerations for, 158-59
  marriage and family issues, 160-62
  renewing relationship with sibling with autism, 157-58
  roles of, 71, 152-57
  support for, 165-66
  unresolved emotions of, 22
Aggression, 63, 69, 138. *See also* Tantrums
Applied behavior analysis, 7, 134. *See also* Behavior management
ARC, 118, 169

Asperger's disorder, 163
Asperger Syndrome Coalition, 169
Attention, parental, 105-06, 107-08
Autistic children. *See* Children with autism
Autism
  broaching the subject of, 48-49
  causes of, 161
  ignorance about, 56
  recognized as disorder, 150
  siblings' understanding of, 34-47
Autism Society Canada, 170
Autism Society of America, 74, 118, 119, 134, 160, 169
Babysitters, 109, 116
Baker, Bruce, 145
Bank, Stephen, 8
Behavior Analyst Certification Board, 170
Behavior analysts, 7, 63, 134
Behavior, changes in, 92
Behavior management, 130-32, 134
Behavioral Intervention for Young Children with Autism, 133
Behaviors, autistic, 58-59, 61, 68-69, 90-91, 114
Bibace, Roger, 32
Birth order, 14
Books, personalized, 60-61
Brothers, younger, 14

Case studies
  Garcia brothers, 149-50
  Gonzalez family, 103-04
  Jansen family, 53-54
  Laurel family, 127-28
  Martin family, 79-81
  McGuire family, 1-3
  Schaefer family, 27-28
"Catching" autism. See Contagion
Celiberti, David, 129, 131
Child care. See Babysitters; Respite
Childbearing concerns, 161-62, 163
Children with autism
  and tolerance of change, 112
  communication skills of, 90
  emotions of, 89, 90
  in adolescence, 136
  including in activities, 107-09
  needs of, for consistency, 131
  others' reactions to, 54, 55
  play skills of, 18, 129-30
  teaching about autism, 49-50, 73-74
Children with Autism (book), 74
Chores, 115-16
Cognitive development, 28
Commands. See Instructions
Communication
  alternative forms of, 90
  between siblings, 90
  between spouses, 88-89
  difficulties in, 3, 28, 85-88
  importance of, 82
  strategies to encourage, 49,91-97
Concrete operational stage, 31, 33-34
Consistency, 131
Contagion, 33, 38-39, 41, 60
Contamination, 33
Counseling, 5, 6-7, 69, 70, 89, 97, 166
Darling, Rosalyn, 16
Destruction of property, 114
Developmental stages, 31-32, 57-58
Diabetes, 29-30

Diagnostic and Statistical Manual, 150
Directions. See Instructions
Discipline, 69, 114. See also
  Behaviors, autistic
Down syndrome, 15
Echolalia, 56
El-Ghoroury, Nabil, 129
E-mail, 120
Emotions of parents, 85-86, 94-96
Emotions of siblings
  accepting, 96-97
  affirming, 93-94
  anger, 17, 20, 22, 56, 60
  anxiety, 15
  dealing with, 61-62
  depression, 15
  embarrassment, 19, 66, 69, 110
  feeling less loved, 105, 106-07
  fear, 56, 59
  frustration, 3, 13
  guilt, 19, 56, 60
  jealousy, 3, 17, 56, 60, 105
  related to parents' emotions, 85-86
  resentment, 13, 17, 19
  shame, 3, 17, 69
Family activities, 107-09, 110-12
Family conferences, 98-99
Family therapists, 6
Family Village website, 120, 170
Fantasy, 60
Feelings. See Emotions
Financial planning, 158-59
Fitting in, 65-66
Formal operational stage, 31-32, 34
Foster parents, 5
Genetic counselor, 69
Glasberg, Beth, 35, 122
Grandparents, 117
Guardians, 159
Harris, Sandra, 129, 131
Illness, children's understanding of,
  29-30, 32-34

Incomprehension, 33
Independence, siblings', 64-65, 70-71
Information about autism
  for children with autism, 49-50
  for siblings, 16-18, 48, 58-61, 63-65
  when to offer, 56-57, 64, 70
  withholding, 87
Institutionalization, 151
Instructions, 138-40
Internalization, 33-34
Internet, 119-20
Kahn, Michael, 8
Kanner, Leo, 150
Learning problems, siblings', 6-8, 98
Listening, 91-92
Lobato, Debra, 121
Love, parental, 105, 106-07
Magical thinking, 60
McHale, Susan, 14
Mental retardation, 14, 18, 63, 89,
  129, 136, 145
Meyer, Don, 121
Mothers, 105
National Autism Society, 170
Neurologists, 6
Online resources, 119-20
Parents. *See also* Spouses
  adoptive, 5
  as fallible human beings, 66-67
  as partners in child's education,
    131
  communication between, 88-89
  death of, 72
  disabilities in, 6
  emotions of, 85-86, 94-96
  overestimation of children's
    knowledge, 47
  qualities of effective, 10-11
  role of in supporting children, 12
  single, 5, 122
  support groups for, 119-20
  withholding information, 87

Peers, 65-66
Phenomenism, 33, 40
Physiological reasoning stage, 34
Piaget, Jean, 28-31
Picture Exchange Communication
  System (PECS), 90
Play skills, 129-46
Powers, Michael, 74
Praise, 138, 140-41
Preoperational stage, 31, 32-33, 43
Privacy, 112-14
Prompts, 130, 133, 139, 142-43
Protection & Advocacy, 160, 170
Psycho-physiological reasoning
  stage, 34
Psychologists
  clinical, 6
  school, 7
  support provided by, 69, 70, 134
Psychiatrists, 6
Puppets, 62
Reaching Out, Joining In, 112
Reading difficulties, 6
Reinforcement, 120
Respite, 69, 109, 118-19
Responsibilities
  inequitable division of, 19-20
Rewards, 130, 133, 140-42
Right from the Start, 133, 145
Role reversal, 19
Romanczyk, Raymond, 129
Safety, 62-63
Seligman, Milton, 16
Sibling relationships
  and new baby, 9-10
  changes with age, 10
  characteristics of strong, 8-9
  effects of age differences, 8, 10
  in adulthood, 12
  in early childhood, 9-11, 14
  in middle childhood and
    adolescence, 11-12

Sibling rivalry, 9
Sibling support groups, 97, 120-22,
    162, 166
Sibling Support Project, 166, 171
Siblings, of children with autism. *See
    also* Adult siblings; Emotions of
    siblings
    as teachers, 131-34, 145
    behavior changes in, 92
    birth order of, 14
    caretaking responsibilities of, 18-20
    concerns of, 22-23
    contrasted with other siblings,14-16
    counseling for, 97
    developmental disorders in, 6-8,
        98
    difficulties seeing self as
        individual, 17
    independence of, 64-65
    information needs of, 16-18, 48,
        56-61, 63-64
    needs of, for free time, 113
    needs of, for parental attention,
        107-09
    prognosis for, 13
    safety of, 62-63
    self-esteem of, 15
    support groups for, 97, 120-22,
        162, 166
    understanding of autism, 34-47
Sibnet, 166, 170
Sibshops, 121
Sign language, 90
Single parents, 5, 122
Sisters, older, 14, 18
Social stories, 112
South Carolina Department of
    Disabilities and Special Needs, 166
Special education teachers, 7
Speech delays, siblings', 6
Spouses
    communication between, 88-89

need for time alone, 109
Stepparents, 5
Steps to Independence, 133
Stories. *See* Books, personalized
Support, sources of, 116-22. *See also*
    Sibling support groups
Tantrums, 59, 62-63,138. *See also*
    Behaviors, autistic
Teenagers. *See* Adolescent siblings
Toys, 135-36
Teachers
    role of, in behavior management, 69
    special education, 7
Touch, resistance to, 143
Vadasy, Patricia, 121
Walsh, Mary, 32

ABOUT THE AUTHORS

Sandra L. Harris, Ph.D., is a Board of Governors Distinguished Service Professor at the Graduate School of Applied and Professional Psychology and the Department of Psychology at Rutgers, The State University of New Jersey. She is the Founder and Executive Director of the Douglass Developmental Disabilities Center at Rutgers. The Center serves people with autism and their families from preschool through adulthood.

Beth A. Glasberg, Ph.D., is Research Assistant Professor and Assistant Director of the Division of Research and Training at Douglass Developmental Disabilities Center at Rutgers. She is a Board Certified Behavior Analyst and two-time recipient of The Lebec Prize for Research in Autism.